BOGORODITZA

She Who Gave Birth to God

Catherine deHueck Doherty

MADONNA HOUSE   PUBLICATIONS
Combermere, Ontario   Canada   K0J 1L0

Original painting on cover by: Nori Peter

Lettering on cover and chapter dividers:
                                    Betty Biesenthal, Design House
Sketch used on chapter dividers: Nicholas Makletzoff
Compiled by: Linda Lambeth

Canadian Cataloguing in Publication Data
Doherty, Catherine de Hueck 1896-1985

BOGORODITZA
She Who Gave Birth to God

ISBN 0-921440-48-0

1. Mary, Blessed Virgin, Saint—Theology.
2. Catholic Church—Doctrines. I. Title.

BT602.D64 1998   232.91   C98-900143-1

Madonna House Publications
Combermere, Ontario
K0J 1L0

Printed in Canada

Dedication

to the Pioneers of Madonna House

Note on shrine
The shrine depicted on the front cover
and chapter dividers is the Russian shrine
on Catherine's "island" in Combermere.
(See text pp. 22-23.)

Table of Contents

Foreword

In the later years of her life Catherine had a burning desire to write a book on Our Lady; a book that she felt was so needed to bring Our Lady into the heart of our lives. Before Catherine could complete her dream she entered into her last illness. It is significant that in the twilight of her life it was Our Lady she wanted to give us. She wanted with all her heart to show us that we have a Mother.

Bogoróditza gathers up material from Catherine's writings throughout her life: from her joyous childhood to the intense suffering of the Russian Communist Revolution and her flight as a refugee; from her broken marriage and the stirrings of her strange new vocation, to her total commitment to serve the poor, and the founding of first Friendship House, and later Madonna House.

Catherine had a favorite prayer: "Give me the heart of a child, and the awesome courage to live it out." It is well to read this book with the heart of a child. That is the way Catherine wrote it. She was born with the heart of a child and retained that grace to the end. We all desire the grace of living our lives with such a heart. It does take awesome courage to do it. Catherine had that courage.

In speaking of her relationship with the Mother of God Catherine said: "*Mary is my life.* I hope I never have any other, for my life is passed under the finely wrought posts of her Gate. Some day the Gate will open, and she will lead me to her Son.

"In the meantime I shall wait at the posts of her Gate, seeking to mold my life ever more unto hers, dwelling in her holy silence and Motherly love."

It is our hope that this work fulfills Catherine's dream. She is no longer with us to do it herself. But she is with us in a far greater way than she could ever have been on earth. She will pray for us as we walk through these pages.

—The Editor

Introduction

Desperately we seek happiness. The majority of us understand that happiness is found in love. But today the way we use the word "love" often misses its very essence. As humanity is losing its sense of its own identity, it is losing its understanding of love as well, and the pursuit of what many think of as love doesn't bring the fulfilment that they expect. Perhaps it is because love has been equated with lust, with encounters that barely touch the hearts of those who casually have met and as casually parted.

Yes, we seek happiness and dimly know that love is happiness, but we have lost the true meaning of love. We are going around seeking it or seeking someone who can tell us where it is to be found.

One person who can direct us to love is Mary, the Mother of God. She became pregnant with the Son of God, the Incarnation of Love and gave him birth! She bore him, brought him up, watched him grow to manhood. She lived with him, followed him at a distance, and stood under his cross as he made his supreme sacrifice out of love for the whole human race.

Mary knows the way of Love intimately, deeply, and profoundly. Of all the people who have ever lived, Mary is the one through whom Love was born.

To go to Mary, as you would go to a beloved neighbor's house, to sit down in her kitchen, and to ask her to tell you about Love and the way to it, is the simplest thing in the world! For to a Christian with faith in the communion of saints, relationships span time and extend into eternity. Those who have died are with us, and we are with them, united in the immense bond of Love that is the Lord. And so talking to Mary should be very simple. Many have found the way easily. More should try.

She will tell you about her Son who took upon himself your pain and my pain, your sin and mine. She will tell you about the deep, strange, fantastic obedience he had to his Father, and we will know what obedience truly is, and how to pave the way to Love. She will explain that to be fulfilled and find our identity, we have to drop the pronoun "I" and live by a total attention, by constant listening to him, to her—to the other.

She will explain that no one should really do "their thing" selfishly, but should open their heart and embrace "all good things" that the other does.

Lastly, she will speak in a low voice about her own *fiat*, her simple "yes" to God. And if we listen carefully to the gentle voice of the mother of Jesus, we will know what that "yes" means in our life. We will know what Love is and, having found it, we will never let it go. So let us turn to this woman who can truly liberate us.

—Catherine de Hueck Doherty

Mama Maria

1

Mama Maria

Before I could speak any language properly, when I was just a little child, I knew Mary.

Her icon, a holy picture of her, hung in my parents' bedroom. It was ancient and dark with time, but sparkling with family gems, offerings of petitions and gratitude. Except on Good Friday, a lampada (vigil light) burned before it always. It was not the candle-shaped kind seen in the West, but one filled with blessed oil, on which a little cork held the wick that seemed to burn more warmly and evenly than any other I have ever seen.

Svitáya Bogoróditza—Maria—Blagodátnaya. These were the names given to her by my parents. "Holy, She Who Gave Birth to God, Maria filled with the fullness of grace." Such would be the literal translation of these strange words. Yet to my early days she was just "Maria, our Mother," my mother's mother, my father's mother, my brother's mother, my mother, everybody's mother. How could it be otherwise? For when my parents went out in the evening they brought me, all warm and cozy and half asleep after my evening bath, to her icon, and prayed that she might take care of the house and me while they were gone.

If I was naughty it was not enough to apologize to Mother and Father, or whomever else I had to apologize to. Off I was sent to apologize to Maria. She would present my apologies to her divine Son, who would accept them so much more readily from her hands. This was, of course, beyond me at the time, and I just said, "Sorry, Mama Maria." But as time went on, I understood more how right and proper that was.

If there was joy in the house, the joy of a great feast day, trip, vacation, or one's own feast day (in Russia these are celebrated in preference to birthdays), or any other kind of good fortune, it was of the essence to share it with Mama Maria by leaving some candles or a new toy on the little table before her icon (where Mother always kept some flowers or plants). She would offer these joys to her divine Son. For sorrow and joy, pain, repentance, and all things of life came to us, her earthly children, from him through her hands, to be given back to him through her, as gifts of our love.

We were so poor! We had nothing to give but what we received. And, naturally, even gifts and all nice things we liked had to be "shared" with her Son, through her. He and Mary would then give these things to the poor children. For unless we "shared" all things with God and his gracious mother—through the poor—how could we ever hope to see them after death? For hadn't Christ said, "Whatsoever you do to the least of my brothers you do to me" (Mt 25:40)? It was never too early to start that sharing.

Thus, slowly, naturally, imperceptibly, "Mama Maria" entered my life and permeated it. She was there when I awoke, as I gave my day to her for her Son. She was there when I went to school; learning (even arithmetic, which I disliked) had one goal only—to get knowledge, all kinds of knowledge, that I might better know and love and serve her Son. She was the best teacher ever, so just saying "Maria" would help.

It was good to know that she was close. She was there in our children's games. She brought her Son to play with us, or so it seemed. And later it was quite clear that she watched us. There were moments in early and late youth when my brothers or I would like to hide from her motherly eye and grasp this forbidden fruit or that, but there she was! How could you get rid of her? And if you tried, as children will try, there always was the comforting security of deep, deep faith. Maria, mother of sinners, was close and would help me to pick myself up!

Years passed. Tragedy came into my life, seemingly without end. I entered the immense domain of Lady Pain—war and revolution, the atheistic communist one, came to me, mine, and Holy Russia.

Then Maria came into her own in my life. Because I knew her, because my life was lived from babyhood within her radiant shadow, because my feet had followed her through every Joyful Mystery of the Rosary, it was only natural that I turned to her when the Sorrowful Mysteries of our faith came into my life.

Gethsemane became a reality for me. I saw my loved ones led one by one to slaughter, arrested, imprisoned unjustly, executed summarily; while I myself lived under the exhausting mental sufferings of waiting, waiting for the same fate to overtake me. Finally, the blow fell, and I knew imprisonment and clearly saw the face of death.

I was condemned to die by hunger, which reduced my body to weakness and blanketed my mind with terror, and God receded until it seemed he was not there, and I was lying in the dust of the thousand endless converging roads of near despair. Is it any wonder that Our Mother came then, and, taking me by the hand, walked once more the Way of the Cross, this time with me and with thousands of my compatriots as she had done with her own Son?

Half delirious with hunger, weakness, and mental pain, I still remember repeating, like a refrain, one word: Maria—Maria—Maria. In it was the only light in my stygian darkness. In it was the only strength that kept me from going over the thin, icy, cold edge of despair. In it was benediction and oil to my wounds. In it was more, for in her, the gate to the Way that is Christ, the daughter of the Father, in whom he is well pleased, the spouse of the Holy Spirit, the Crimson Dove of Love, lies the secret of Uncreated Light, the secret of our hope in hopelessness.

She, the shelter of the shelterless, the House of Gold, opened the door to me and allowed me to enter, and once I had entered, to understand that no one is tried beyond her capacity. She, the mediatrix of all graces, the one through whom Christ gives all graces, will bring graces enough and more to every Christian. Thus we will be enabled to say that *fiat* which each of us must say before the mystery of the Cross when it is our turn to lie and be nailed upon it!

The mother of joy brought joy into my desert of pain and death. Through her fragrant love, she showed me the way to Love Incarnate, her Son, and made my Calvary acceptable, even infinitely desirable, through his. She brought the radiance of his peace to shine on me in the midst of Satan's un-peace.

She took my spirit into her blessed hands, and just as my own mother used to lift me up when I was a child for her nightly blessing, so now Mary lifted me up for the blessing of the Father, the Son, and the Holy Spirit. Or so it seemed to my exhausted mind and body, into which flowed a new and strong life of faith and hope and love.

Years later, when all these dark days of earthly hell were but a memory, I understood that she who had walked with me to all my schools, had finally taken me into her own school of holy silence and love.

Is it any wonder, then, that today the lay apostolate of Madonna House—first founded in 1930 as Friendship House, in Toronto, Canada—has since spread across the world? It is solidly built on the foundation that the Lord himself chose for his coming to us.

Blagodátnaya Maria is indeed the real foundress of Madonna House. All its field houses are, I hope, but the beginning of our own joyous litany of her most beloved name. Those whose glorious vocation it is to staff these houses in her service and that of her divine Son are totally consecrated to her. Fervently we pray that these, her houses of divine love, may be beacons of light in this dark world, bringing his light into it.

Mary is my life. I hope I never have any other, for my life is passed under the finely wrought posts of her gate. Some day the gate will open, and she will lead me to her Son.

In the meantime I shall wait at the posts of her gate, seeking to mold my life ever more unto hers, dwelling in her holy silence and motherly love.

Holy Mother Russia

2

Holy Mother of Russia

Bogoróditza—She Who Gave Birth to God! That is what the Russians call the Blessed Mother.

Legend has it that this title was first used by the beautiful Russian queen, St. Olga, who in 955 journeyed across the sea to be baptized by the Patriarch of Constantinople.

Olga, widow of Igor, was at the time regent of the Russian kingdom. Influenced by the few Christians already in the country, she sought baptism for herself and then devoted her life to the conversion of her people.

Be that as it may, when the faith was introduced into Russia, devotion to the Mother of God came with it. And despite schism and revolution, love of the Blessed Virgin rules the hearts of the Russian people to this day.

Russia's devotion to Mary grew with the nation. Its history can be read in the litany of titles given to her. For wherever the Russians went, she seemed to go ahead of them, appearing miraculously now in this plain, now in that city or stronghold, showering them with blessings.

And each time, some solitary artist in some hidden monastery would record these happenings with an icon, a holy picture, of the Bogoroditza. Thus, we have the Holy Virgin of Kazan, the Blessed Mother of Czestochowa, the

Bogoroditzas of Kiev, of Tver, and of Novgorod. And with each icon are stories of miracles like those of Fatima and Lourdes.

Like a gossamer fabric, shining, light but infinitely strong, She Who Gave Birth to God permeated every fiber, every nook, every corner of the Russian land, its people and their lives. Someday historians and artists will discover this and reveal to the world the rosary of Russian shrines dedicated just to her. For there was no city too big, no hamlet too small in that immense land, where some landmark, shrine, or icon had not been made and erected in her honor.

It was she who originally got the scattered sections of Russia acquainted with one another. For Russians, like the rest of her children the world over, turned to her for almost all the favors they wanted to ask from her Son. And in petition for her intercession, or in gratitude for favors received, they went on distant pilgrimage to her many shrines.

They went fasting, barefoot, and simply clad, chanting her litanies along the way. The Russian is acutely aware of the importance of fasting and penance in seeking God's favor through her intercession. It is a remedy given by God himself to untie the hands of his mercy and appease the demands of his justice.

Through these constant pilgrimages, men, women, and children of every social stratum came together praising her name, learning to love her and her Son, learning to love one another.

There are many icons in every traditional Russian home, but Mary's icon always hangs in the eastern corner of the bedroom. A gently flickering vigil light burns before it night and day down through the years. The life of the family starts and ends here. It is to her that the bridegroom brings his bride. Together they kneel before her gentle face and ask her benediction on their marital love, begging her to make it fruitful in her Son, the Lord. It is to her they pray again when their love has been consummated, thanking her for the infinite blessing of cooperating with God in his work of creation, and praying for a child which, then and there, they dedicate to her and her Son. For is she not the mother of him who is the Giver of Life?

It is before this icon that the mother prays during childbirth. It is before her that the new-born child is brought for a blessing and later kneels and prays all his little prayers. Family councils are held before her and it is she again who receives the last death-whisper of father, mother, or child. She is the center of the life of the household.

An old and revered custom is to remember Mary in one's will. Tsars and commoners, princes and paupers, have willed their best to her, either in the shape of money, precious stones, or silver and gold. That is why most of the well-known icons in Russian churches are so richly decorated. Each stone, each gold leaf, each silver bit, represents either thanks for favors received or petitions for the same.

Those who have no riches bring her the work of their hands. Her shrines, usually small chapels, or special altars in bigger churches, are decorated with exquisitely embroidered silks and linens that take years to make. Fruits and plants are temporary gifts to her from grateful farmers.

The old Russian greeting starts with, "May the peace of God be with you." But the farewell is Mary's: "May the blue mantle of Our Lady cover you with its gracious folds and keep you safe."

Mary permeates the liturgy. She fills its many *Ektenias* (litanies), she walks through the Mass, she is invoked at the *Panikhida*, the prayer for the dead, and she is present in the *Moleben,* the prayer of petition. There are many songs about her, liturgical and national.

It is her icon that blesses the child. Parental blessings are a must for all occasions in Russian life: for school, for sickness, for marriage, for a new job. It is Mary's picture that the father and mother use in giving them.

The Hail Mary is the prayer that the Russians like best. (They say it differently from Western Christians: they use the complete form of the first half, "Hail Mary, full of grace," but omit the second half, "Holy Mary, Mother of God.")

It was devotion to Mary as the mother of Christ and of all humanity that preserved in Russia the doctrine of the Mystical Body. You see this sublime doctrine reflected in the giants of Russian literature, Dostoevsky, Tolstoy, Chekhov and, if the truth be told, even in many present day writers. The hunger for justice is the most characteristic trait of the Russian. In his eternal quest for the realization of the ideal of the Mystical Body, he may wander into heresy, even the heresy of communism.

But he will not stay there long, as God reckons time. How could he, when he loves God's mother so well? Mary herself, at Fatima, promised that Russia would one day be restored. At one time, with East and West divided, this seemed, humanly speaking, impossible. But nothing is impossible to God's grace.

It may be a long time until true freedom of religion exists in Russia. But the leaven of divine grace is always at work. Some day the promise of Fatima will be fulfilled and the nation Russia will once again be within the fold of Peter.

Not until that day will the world know the peace for which it so ardently yearns. For peace can come only with unity of spirit, not just of leagues and alliances. Such unity can be achieved only by prayer, the prayer of God-fearing men and women all over the world.

And to whom should we pray but the Bogoroditza, She Who Gave Birth to God? She loves Russia, and Russia, even the former Soviet Russia, has always loved her. It is to her that we must pray, that she will cover the Russians with the blue mantle of her love and carry them in its gracious folds back to their Father's house.

Millions of Russians, exhausted by long years of war and revolution and disillusioned by the empty promises of a materialist state, pray to her daily for that end. Will you join me and them in this prayer?

My Russian Shrine

The men of Madonna House built a shrine for me, the kind seen in Russia. Currently the government in Russia is beginning to preserve them as historical monuments. My Russian shrine was built and blessed for the opening of the Second Vatican Council. A vigil light has burned there continuously up to this day, for the unity of the Church East and West. The icon of Our Lady is there. There is also a bidding towel—a towel with a symbol of a bidding prayer (a prayer request) embroidered on it. The family member who asks their wife or mother or sister to embroider their needs into it takes it, when finished, to the parish priest, who blesses it and puts it over the icon. The bidding towel in our Russian corner in Madonna House was embroidered by my mother. She must have wanted a good garden because she embroidered flowers on it. The bidding towel in my Russian Shrine is for vocations to our apostolate. Two men and two women are embroidered on it. (There is a representation of this shrine, including the bidding towel, on the front cover of this book.)

To explain who Our Lady is to us is almost impossible. Scripturally you could say that she's the gate—the gate to the Father, because it is through her that we return to him. Every Russian understands that. Our Lady is our breath. It is our life. If I stop breathing, I die.

Apparitions

3

Apparitions

Truths to Believe

From the very day of the first Pentecost, Mary the Mother of God was loved and venerated in the Church.

Although she appears from the Gospels to have spoken very little, St. Luke brought her to the forefront in his Gospel. The Fathers of the Church, giants of wisdom, grace, sanctity, and knowledge, unfolded resplendently the place she occupied in the slowly developing theology of the Church.

The shepherds of Church spoke with infallible voice proclaiming truths regarding the Virgin Mother. These truths are to be believed by all calling themselves Catholic, by all members of the Mystical Body of Christ, the Church.

Majestically, led by the hand of her spouse the Holy Spirit, Mary emerged from the deep, holy shadows of her silence and effacement, revealing aspects of the truth of who she is as our minds were ready to accept them.

Along with this inner spiritual unfolding, Mary showed herself in a series of apparitions until, clear and perfect, she stood revealed to the gaze of her human children as the mother she is!

This century has been called the Marian age. Mary, the woman clothed in silence, has become so articulate in her many apparitions, and our knowledge of her has taken its full place in the theology and the dogma of the Church.

We must study the messages expressed in her apparitions, and in our studying understand that each one calls us to repentance, prayer, mortification and conversion of heart. Then the love and mercy of God will become apparent to us in its immensity and its infinite depths, as having brought Mary to us, her children once lost to her Son, the Way and the Truth.

Although she spent her time on earth cloaked in silence, she is speaking to us today, from the shrines of Lourdes, Fatima, and many other places. If we only take time out to listen, and to ponder her words, our century will be a century of peace, our lives will be lives of joy. Instead, we go about harassed and worried by wars and rumors of wars, facing eternally a twilight of our own making, when, for the lifting up of our faces and hearts, we could have the vision of God and his peace!

Why not begin a journey inward to the Immaculate Heart of Mary, to learn from her the secret of the King, her Son, the secret that would change our lives, and with them, the life of the whole world.

Ever the compassionate one, our constant intercessor, she has pleaded our cause before God throughout the history of the Church. She has received reprieve after reprieve for us.

But the reprieve was not without conditions. Prayer and mortification have been asked of us according to our state in life in the world. Have we complied? Is our compliance so evident that a new spirit is flooding the world? A spirit of sorrow for our sins? A spirit of reparation to the most Sacred Heart of her Son, so deeply wounded by sin?

What of our spirit of prayer? Is it lifting us and the world with us in a storm of supplication and love to the feet of the Father? Are our churches so crowded that morning and night there is standing room only?

The answer seems negative. And the world is hurtling even faster and faster to its strange doom.

Yet, as we watch the face of the gentle Virgin, she seems to change! Slowly, she grows in stature. Slowly, the sun clothes her in its brilliancy. Humbly, the moon moves to become her footstool. And stars arrange themselves, trembling, to form a crown of surpassing beauty around her regal head.

Now indeed she has become the Queen of Heaven and the Universe, and her face begins to reflect the holy anger of the Father, who folds the hands of his mercy and begins to loose the hands of his justice. Is she to be the spear of that justice? Is she to be the fiery arrow of his bow, this woman clothed with the sun, the moon beneath her feet and stars for a crown? (Rv 12:1). If she is, then woe is to us. For indeed she is more powerful than an army in battle array; she is the mother of the forgotten God, the God mocked, despised, and denied.

Let it never come to pass that we have the Virgin most powerful against us because we have not heeded her gentle pleadings, her miraculous apparitions, her constant and besieging requests, which she made because she loved us so.

She never spoke a useless word. Silence was her dwelling. Silence was her cloak. Silence was her companion. That is why her words carry the immense weight of incarnated truth. It behooves us to listen to them and to implement them in our daily lives!

The Woman Who Weeps

One image I have of Our Lady weeping is that of Our Lady of Salette. La Salette is a small town in southeastern France where she appeared to two children in 1846. She appeared sitting on a large rock, her face in her hands, weeping.

I have never been to La Salette or to Lourdes, though I have been to Fatima. I loved Fatima. I saw it when it was still a wild place. I made a pilgrimage on foot and slept under a tree. That was back in 1937.

I love Lourdes from afar, for I love everything about Our Lady; and every one of her apparitions approved by the Church pierces my heart. I take her words to heart. I know that I don't have to, for private revelations, even of this tremendous type, are not binding on Christians.[*] But I hope my heart is childlike. I believe in miracles so I take every one of Our Lady's to heart.

I first came to know Our Lady of Salette in Léon Bloy's book, *The Woman Who Was Poor.* She affected me deeply, because I, too, had wept. I had wept at having lost my country, all that I possessed, and many of my close relatives in the Communist Revolution. I knew to a small degree what Our Lady knew when Simeon told her that a sword would pierce her heart.

A country is not a son, but seeing my country ravaged, as Russia was, was somewhat like being at the crucifixion of one most dear. So I understood her who wept just a tiny bit more than I would have otherwise. I cannot get rid of the

---

[*] For the teaching of the Church on apparitions see *Catechism of the Catholic Church,* § 67.

image of the Mother of God weeping over her children, the whole human race.

Later on in my life I came to a crossroads. Today I know it was the crossroads of my destiny; that in his infinite mercy, God had chosen me to become a foundress of a lay apostolate. Then I did not know this. But I knew something else! I knew with my whole heart, my whole soul, and perhaps even my body, that I had to console her who weeps on the mountain of La Salette!

It seemed to me that I had to go up there somehow, even if only in some symbolic way; that I had to take her hands away from her face; that I had to wipe away her tears.

How could I do that? This was in the 1920s. I was a refugee. I couldn't travel. It was too far. I was too poor. And could a young woman move hands as of stone? No, that wasn't the answer.

I loved her Son passionately. I wanted to serve him with my whole heart and soul. Also, I wanted to console her who weeps. She haunted my days and nights. Perhaps I realized that consoling her involved consoling her divine Son and serving him better, since the reason she wept over us, her children, was that we did not heed his voice, did not turn our face to the Father, did not allow the Holy Spirit to guide us.

Then it came to me. I *could* wipe away those tears. I *could* separate those hands that covered her face. Perhaps I could even take her in my arms and whisper into her ear the things that women whisper when they have someone to console.

I could do all that by doing it in my neighbor! All I had to do was follow her Son's injunction to sell all that I possessed, take up my cross, and follow him.

I did this and it led me into the slums of the big cities of Canada and the United States. It led me into the darkest and strangest streets and alleys of Harlem, the city within New York City where the Black dwelt in segregation. It led me to many slums of many cities, and even to the strange, hidden poverty in the backwoods and rural areas of Canada.

Today my spiritual sons and daughters, the priests, laymen, and laywomen of Madonna House Apostolate, are led all over the world. There are many young people who go to her and open the hands of her who weeps. Many young hands wipe away her tears. And I am consoled too!

I have never been to La Salette. Yet I live there. I love Our Lady under many names. I have written about her in many ways. But dominating my thoughts, urging me on, is forever the bowed figure of the woman who weeps, the woman who is the Mother of God.

We speak a lot today about training laypeople in the apostolate of Christ, and also the training of priests and religious. (Or is the word re-training?)

We need re-training. We need to open our hearts and learn to listen with them. We need to beg God for his precious gift of tears, that we may wash ourselves clean of our sins of omission and commission, and also wash the world.

We must learn to love and to serve better. Who is going to teach us? Our Lady of La Salette, whose tears flow constantly over us.

Perhaps her tears are the reason our world still exists. This I wouldn't know. One thing I do know. I love her with a great love, and I sit at her feet always. Whatever I know about her Son, she has taught me. If there is a Madonna House Apostolate today, it is because Our Lady once wept on the mountain of La Salette.

Our Lady of La Salette, pray for us, your children. Lead us to your Son. Help us to dry your tears, for one of your tears is heavier on the soul of each of us than the weight of the whole world. We need you so desperately to teach us how to weep cleansing tears.

Our Lady of La Salette, pray for us.

Controversial
Figure

4

A Controversial Figure

Nothing to Fear

Incredible as this may seem, Mary, the Mother of God, has become a controversial figure! Learned theologians and biblical scholars have written and spoken millions of words about her in their books, lectures, and the other media. They are listened to eagerly, often reverently. But they prove, at times, to be a little too learned for everyone to understand. Rumors reach the laity from everywhere, some confirmed, some unconfirmed, some clarifying, others confusing ordinary minds. There is a feeling in the air, (a mistaken one, of course), that due to the new ecumenical spirit, Our Lady is somehow or other being made to take a secondary or different place in the Catholic Church.

To some it seems as if she is being "soft-pedaled" for manifold reasons. Many ordinary "grass roots" Catholics are worried and uneasy about all these happenings. Yet they shouldn't be, for Our Lady is very much in the forefront, still in her rightful place.

All the theologians are trying to do is encourage the laity to be less sentimental about Mary. As examples of "sentimental" devotions, they discuss some old devotions and observances and try to show them as being not in keeping with our times, as "unliturgical," or "paraliturgical."

Many seem to be worried about Mary and the ecumenical movement. She seems suddenly to have become a stumbling block to unity. People, especially the humble, simple people—the majority of humanity in fact, to whom the Gospel should be preached in its fullness—have become more and more confused. As usual, it's mostly due to semantics. For again and again, we see that in a world chock full of old and new ways of communicating we understand each other less and less! (Something like this must have happened during the building of the Tower of Babel. The people then didn't have any "simultaneous electronic communications" such as we have, but they certainly were as confused as so many of us are.)

Be that as it may, Mary could never be a stumbling block to unity. She is the mother of all humankind. She is a wondrous sign of unity among the creatures of God, one of the most wondrous of all!

Let us look at her a little more closely. She is indeed the "woman wrapped in silence," a mystery. Her soul, her heart, and her mind were wrapped in silence. Yet in her everyday life, she was the mother of love, of *caritas*—God. God, who came among us as one of us, with words of wisdom and light. So in this she spoke to us too. She still does. Let us hear her. Let us listen well.

For it was Mary who, through the centuries, helped the ordinary faithful to keep the faith, with or without priests. It was Mary who saw them through lean times and good times, through their pains, sorrows, and joys. In her they found their rest. In her they renewed their courage. Again and again, popes warned theologians, intellectuals, and priestly and lay apostles to be gentle, considerate, and very clear in their explanation of what was happening in the Church regarding Mary. On no account were they to decry the old, familiar devotions and practices that have sustained generations of Catholics through their lives. They were to gently lead the faithful to a true appraisal of Mary's role in the Church and in their lives.

Her task as Mother of God and mother of humans has always been to lead her human children to her divine Son. This she has done through the centuries; this she will do through the coming centuries until the day of the Second Coming of the Lord.

Our Lady is wise beyond human wisdom. And it matters little which ways she uses with her human children to lead them to God. Obviously, each century, and maybe each generation or decade, will require different ways, different approaches. She knows them all, and she will use them all. Therefore, there is nothing to fear. The Church, of which she is a part and a symbol, holds fast to her and will never let go. So no one need fear any decrease in Our Lady's stature, any falling of a shadow on her. No such decrease can happen. No such shadow can fall.

On the contrary, as a result of all this searching, this evaluating and re-evaluating, as a result of the work of the theologians and biblical scholars, Our Lady will emerge in a new splendor. She will emerge cleansed from the little ways and little devotions that ordinary folks lovingly, but perhaps injudiciously, have rendered her, thereby obscuring her beauty and her splendor in the clogging incense of sentimentality.

She will come forth once again, *Theotokos*, the Mother of God, the woman clothed with the sun, with the moon beneath her feet and the stars around her head, more powerful than an army in battle array. She will emerge as she was.

Slowly, inevitably, her splendor will be revealed, as will her beauty and her role in the Christian Church. And eyes that were sealed and hearts that were closed to her will be opened. Far from being a stumbling block to the ecumenical spirit—a spirit that is cleansing the minds of Christians—she, the spouse of the Holy Spirit, will become a bridge of unity, love, and strength.

There is nothing to fear from the new approaches to Mariology, the theology of Mary.

Her Rightful Place

In the Eastern liturgy Mary occupies her rightful place under many names, the litany of which can easily be found in the Office of Praise of the Mother of God, the *Akathist* hymn.

She is the one who gave birth to God, as the Russians say. She is mentioned in the Eastern liturgy before the consecration, because she gave the Body of Christ to us. She is mentioned after the consecration, in gratitude for her "yes" to the will of God. She is called "the Most Excellent Tabernacle for him who is adored by the Seraphim." By her yes, she opened paradise, because this brought forth the Son of God. The Old Testament speaks of her. The New Testament sings of her. The Akathist says of her, "Oh, you, leafy-branched tree, shading the many! Oh you, Mediatrix before the righteous Judge! Oh you, mercy for all those who have sinned! Oh you, robe of the naked who are in bondage!" Every title in the Akathist, or nearly every one, is based on the Scriptures. It is incredible, incomprehensible, to the Eastern Church that, in this age of ecumenism, true devotion to Our Lady can be downgraded.

She was, par excellence, a laywoman, a mother and a spouse, an ordinary woman as far as human eyes could see. Christ came through her, and she will help us, better than anyone else, to find him in the hubbub and noise of our technology, in the confused maze of our immense urban development, in the quiet, silent, dangerous spaces of the universe that we are discovering. For she is the guiding star of creation, the *Bogoróditza*, this woman who has given birth to God. Her name in Russian means just that. One whole sentence in one word.

So let us re-think. Better, let us re-pray our approach to Mary.

*Our Lady
of the Rosary*

5

Our Lady of the Rosary

Across the world from time immemorial, in pagan days and in Christian days, beads have been used in the expression of love, worship, and remembrance of God. They have been called by various names, but they have always been there.

The Eastern rite people use a *chotki,* made of knotted cord, on which they recite the Jesus Prayer: "Lord Jesus Christ, Son of the living God, have mercy on me a sinner." Many religions have beads they use as a help for prayer, to lift their hearts to another world. Catholics use the Rosary.

For many years in Madonna House I sorted the donations that came to us from all over. Among them were many rosaries. Rosaries of every size and description passed through my hands, many worn thin and made holy by someone who recited them over and over again.

While I was sorting, a picture came into my heart. As each bead passed through the hands using them and fell, a prayer rose to God. Where do those beads of prayer fall? Can you locate them? Yes. They fall into the heart of Our Lady, into the heart of her Son. And who knows, they may even reach the lap of God the Father.

I had a picture of the Father picking up bead for bead: the Muslim beads, the Eastern chotki, the Catholic rosary beads, the beads of many religions, each a kind of rosary. He played with them as a child would. For he said, through his Son, that only children will come to heaven. He must be childlike himself.

In those beads, falling one by one, all the pain and joy of the world are enclosed, and all the tenderness of God.

Mary's Answer

Our world remains poised on the edge of an abyss of darkness. I think of scientists in white, working in gleaming laboratories, dissecting the awesome mysteries of the atom. They work in offices that are soundproofed, quiet as tombs, dealing with figures that few mortals understand, but that may spell utter destruction and death, not only to thousands, or millions, but to all humankind. Atom bombs, hydrogen bombs, nuclear weapons, chemical weapons, weapons of mass destruction in the making are in the minds and under the hands of workers in buildings sheeted in secrecy, guarded like fortresses of old.

Outside is a strange, breathless world of men and women who are living, eating, selling, buying, marrying, yet seemingly also waiting, waiting for something fearsome and dark to happen. They are waiting in fear, in insecurity, in trembling, their minds so many vital unseen threads all meeting at one point—those buildings where the figures of death and life are dealt with.

Like the pagan god Moloch of old, the atom—its bomb, its weaponry, its death potential—is draining our lives and souls, robbing us of the peace of God and of our true selves, casting us into a desert, alone.

Yet, the answer is at hand. The solution is close by. Gently, softly, the thread that will lead us out of the labyrinth of our fears, doubts and turmoil is placed into our sinful hands. It will close the abyss, and, touching the atom, make it a servant, and not an avenging god. The answer, the solution, is the Rosary.

The Rosary: so tiny, so seemingly weak, is to be used against the unseen but deadly power unleashed by the human mind. The Rosary, so foolish a weapon against the millions of fists raised by atheistic communism and the millions of hearts turned toward materialism and life itself.

The Rosary, a prayer of babies, youth, men, and women, is so simple that even the illiterate can pray it, so profound that the geniuses have not begun to probe its depths. The Rosary, a simple vocal prayer, can lead us into the realism of the highest mental and contemplative prayer!

The Rosary is an answer to all our fears, to all our unrest, to all our dangers. It finds us everywhere and leads us back from the desert of darkness where we now dwell, where, forever and ever, the prince of darkness tempts us to fall down and adore him. Yes, it is the answer. Our Lady in her many apparitions said so. Especially at Fatima.

Why, then, are we not listening? Why do so many Catholics leave the Rosary unsaid? Why aren't our days filled with endless Rosaries forming a chain to hold our hearts anchored to the heart of God, through Mary his mother?

It is time to begin now to pray the Rosary daily. We must understand that if we do not, our world will perish, and we with it. And those who are left will dwell in the catacombs, perhaps using only the Rosary, their ten fingers, over and over again, and weeping because they know why they are underground.

Oh, let us pray the Rosary now, so that the children of light may continue to dwell in the light of God's sun, so that the world may be restored to Christ, the Son of God.

Centuries of Love

How many centuries of love and prayer brought the Rosary to us in the simple, childlike form we have it today? The hand of God must have slowly fashioned it, as he himself let the beads of years slip to the earth, one by one, each containing within itself his loving care, his providence, his mercy, his justice and his infinite charity, each a gift of his loving-kindness to us.

It grew slowly with the infant Church. How many chanted it throughout Christendom in the days when Christians sought first the kingdom of heaven, knowing that all the rest would be added to them!

When did it become a string of beads? Our Lady must have liked the simplicity that made it available to all —children, youth, and all the ages of men and women, both the learned and unlearned. "The Psalter of Mary" it was called: three times fifty Hail Marys said by anyone in the place of the one hundred and fifty psalms of the Office, in the days when many could not read. And tradition has it that she blessed it and gave it to St. Dominic to give to others. It is a heavenly lasso, perhaps, to entice her wayward children back into her motherly arms!

It is part of so many recent apparitions, in which she has so emphatically told the world, through the lips of children, to pray the Rosary. How slender a thread to hold our disintegrating world up! And yet how strong. It consists of a short string of a crucifix, one large bead, three smaller ones, and then another large one. This short string is attached to a circlet of beads: five *decades,* or sets of one large bead and ten smaller ones.

How childishly simple these beads, made of anything and everything, strung in orderly rows, beginning with the cross. It is her Son's cross, which she never can or will forget. On the crucifix, we recite the Apostles' Creed: "I believe in God, the Father Almighty...." Then on the first large bead, the first Our Father: "Our Father, who art in heaven..."— her Father and ours. The Father who chose her to be the mother of his Son. The Father who is so pleased with her. The Father who made her immaculate, a vessel of predilection. Then on the three small beads three Hail Marys, Gabriel's angelic salutation, "Hail, Mary, full of grace, the Lord is with you..." which forever resounds in her ears. The last large bead for the Glory Be, "Glory be to the Father, and to the Son, and to the Holy Spirit...." She must love that so, she who is Our Lady of the Trinity! And then the measured, evenly recurring Our Father, ten Hail Marys, and Glory Be said for each decade.

While reciting each decade we meditate on a particular *mystery,* or event in her life, as she leads us through the whole of her life, so full of mysteries. Joyful, Sorrowful, and Glorious Mysteries—deep as the seas of eternity. Simple as the smile of a child. Leading us to the very heart of God, through her who gave him his human heart.

Rosaries are held by millions of hands: the chubby ones of babies, the smooth, beautiful, strong and manly hands of youth, the capable and gentle hands of women and men, the gnarled and work-worn hands of the old, the transparent and weak hands of the sick. Sinners and saints hold them, and, letting them pass through their fingers, bead by bead, enter an unspeakably beautiful symphony of love, woven of two prayers—the Hail Mary, given us by an angel; and the Our

Father, revealed by the Son of God. They are music that leads us on to heights uncharted and unknown, to where God dwells.

A promise of salvation and peace! As we pray, we will remember her promise that she will hold our disintegrating world together and will help us restore ourselves and it, to her Son.

Our Life Is a Rosary

Much has been written and will yet be written about the Rosary, that simple, profound, almost unfathomable prayer to the gracious Mother of God, which takes her children again and again on the pilgrimage of her life and her Son's, until, through it, their lives and God's become one.

Still, there is another "rosary" that many of us miss completely. It is the one that opens up right at our feet, day by day, hour by hour, on the road all of us must travel, the road to God. It is a strange rosary. Its mysteries embrace the life of Christ and his mother, in the Mystical Body of his Church. It is the rosary of our own life. Listen:

The Joyful Mysteries

The Annunciation, by the Angel Gabriel to Mary, and Mary's "yes" to the will of God (Lk 1:26-38): Consider a woman. A man. A child. Most of us pray this mystery by living it in some fashion, by surrendering to the will of God in our daily life. For it is the mystery of every family. How different would our homes be, how quickly would many of our social, psychological, financial, and emotional problems be solved, if we blended our whole married life with the first mystery of the Rosary.

The Visitation of Mary to Elizabeth (Lk 1:39-56): Again, this is our life. For all of us "go on visitations"—to our relations, friends, and neighbors. Our motives are rooted in the same motives that took the slender teenaged girl Mary on her long, hazardous journey to see her cousin Elizabeth.

The Nativity, the birth of Our Lord: Consider the birth of the Child, or of any child anywhere—ours or someone else's. The whole concept of children's welfare, education and environment, would become loving, deeply Christian, and filled with understanding if, in each childbirth, we saw Bethlehem and Christ!

The Presentation of the Child Jesus in the Temple by Joseph and Mary (Lk 2:22-38): Here is the best example of broad, complete obedience to duly constituted authority. It is a mystery, specifically to be meditated on by government officials and their people. Nations would be freed of fears if, on the high plane of international relationships, they would make and accept laws as the sinless Mary did when, holding the divine Infant, creator of all things, she submitted herself and him, humbly and obediently, to the Law of her people and her God.

The Finding of Jesus in the Temple by Joseph and Mary after they had searched for him as if lost (Lk 2:41-50): Sorrow and death, separation and loss would become bearable, almost sweet, if we remembered this fifth joyful mystery of the Rosary. If we made it our own, faith would become reality and we would know that in God all separation ends, all loss is retrieved, all sorrows are healed.

The Sorrowful Mysteries

The Agony of Jesus in the Garden (Mt 26:36-46): Is there anyone living who has not been in that Garden of Desolation? How many have never come out of it, or have perished because they chose to be alone there instead of to kneel by the side of the Man of Sorrows who sweat blood for love of them? To pray out our agonies, with Christ and to Christ in this mystery, is to begin to possess that peace he promised—the peace which surpasses all understanding.

The Flagellation, the scourging of Jesus (Mk 15:15): Who of us has not been "flagellated" by sickness, pain, or incredible and harsh trials? Why waste all this wealth? Why not receive it from the hands of God? Accept it, side by side, with his Son. Why not immerse oneself with him, be one with him in this second sorrowful mystery that holds the secret of so many unanswered questions? Let us try. The answers will come.

Jesus is Crowned with Thorns (Mt 27:27-29): Lift your hand and touch your head or your neighbor's, and each will reveal its own "crown of thorns," invisible but real. Poverty, personality problems, work difficulties, loneliness, frustrations, doubts, their name is legion. Tightly woven, the crown is there. How to endure it? How to remove it? The rosary of our own days, which lies ahead at our feet in the dust of our road to God, is there to be prayed with the Rosary of beads, which holds the secrets of life, death, and love.

Jesus Carries His Cross: Need anyone even speak of this? The cross lays heavily at times on all weak, lacerated shoulders. We cannot throw it off. Our life itself is cruciform, whether we wish it to be or not. Yet, if we carry it step by step with Christ, who fell under the weight of his cross, we shall be eased of its heaviness.

The Crucifixion: This too is our lot. To be crucified on the cross of life. Of pain. Of circumstances. Of family. Of a thousand, thousand things. Are we going to be like the saved thief on one side of him or the scoffing one on the other? (Lk 23:39-43). If we pray this darkest mystery of all, we shall know joy incredible and live in the warmth of constant light.

The Glorious Mysteries

The Resurrection: If we bend and pick up the Rosary of our days, and blend it with the Rosary of the lives of Mary and Jesus, we shall experience the resurrection of spirit and of flesh many times on earth. It will be a foretaste of the resurrection to come. Endless are these little resurrections: Recovery from illness. Insoluble problems solved. Oh so many others! *If* we pray.

The Ascension of Jesus into heaven(Acts 1:9-11): Hope of the hopeless. No abyss is so deep, no degradation so complete, that there is no hope for ascension from it. If only those who think all is over and who are tempted to take their lives would pray this mystery well! They would see and touch their own ascension from the depths of despair.

The Descent of the Holy Spirit on Mary and the Apostles on Pentecost (Acts 2:1-4): Constantly, daily, hourly, this mystery takes place. For constantly the Holy Spirit descends into the hearts of the faithful. He enlightens and strengthens us with his divine gifts and graces. Luminous and of beauty unsurpassed is his constant stream of light. Do we use this third glorious mystery in our drab days?

The Assumption of Mary into heaven: Body and soul, she was taken to heaven. So, too, we shall be reunited after the final judgment with our glorified bodies, in joy everlasting. But even now, today, tomorrow, day by day, we live this mystery. The mere thought that one of us, a creature, is there before the face of the living, uncreated God changes our attitude to our own flesh. What an influence it would be on writers and on all who produce, if all of us prayed, meditated, and made this glorious mystery our own.

Mary Crowned is Queen of Heaven: We are not alone. Our days are not gray, drab, useless. We have a woman of flesh and blood, a queen who was a creature just like us. Now is the moment to bend into the dust of our spiritual road and to lift the Rosary of our whole lives, day by day, into her queenly hands. It will be safe there, as safe as we ourselves will be, if we are her own. She will transform our days with her love and care and, in turn, give them to God. Then we shall see God, and be one with him.

Yes, much has been written about that simple, profoundly unfathomable prayer, and much will yet be written. But better than all writings is the praying of it. It leads us into the book of eternal life.

Teach Us to Pray

Mary, teach us to pray! For see, you who are our mother and the mother of God, somewhere along the dark road of the past decades, while we walked between war and uneasy peace, we have forgotten how to pray.

Show us, O Mother of Wisdom, the height, the depth, the width, and the endless breadth that is to be found in the Rosary. Indeed, it is your song and your prayer.

We need you, Gate of Heaven, to teach us how to pray. Bend down to our littleness and say the Rosary with us. In our spiritual childhood, the beads will teach us how to pray with your voice. In our spiritual youth, through you, they will reveal to us how to plunge our minds into the blessed mystery spelled out by each decade. And in our spiritual maturity, show us your secret ways to the prayer of silence, of contemplation. Your psalter, the Rosary, is a school of prayer and you are the perfect mistress of it.

We stand between war and peace; we live in insecurity and fear; we bear the almost unendurable heat of a market place from which your Son has been almost completely shut out. We truly need to learn how to pray.

Only through prayer can we begin to truly know him whom we must love and serve. If we don't, we will perish. Only through prayer can we *be* before his face and get the strength to then *do,* or to live before him, witnessing, if need be, unto death, to his divinity and to our Christianity. This century needs Christians who are Christians in faith and deed. On such depends the fate of the world.

You who are the gate to Christ, the way to the Father, our ultimate goal, you, Mary, Mother of Christ, teach us to pray your Rosary as it should be prayed. For these ordinary beads strung on threads, hold within themselves all the mysteries of our holy faith and all the main ways of prayer. Mary, Queen of the Rosary, open to us its holy secrets. Let it be our door to the heart of your Son, his Father, and the Holy Spirit.

Total
Consecration

6

Total Consecration

Mary in My Life

On the Feast of Our Lady's Purification, February 2, 1951, I finished a long journey. Or perhaps I should say that I completed the first stage of it. I cannot tell for sure. Time alone will give the final answer.

My journey ended at the feet of Our Lady's altar, in the church of the Sacred Heart in Ottawa, Canada, where my husband, Eddie Doherty, and I consecrated ourselves to her, according to the *True Devotion* of St. Louis Marie de Montfort. On that day we handed over to her all of ourselves, our earthly goods, our spiritual merits and good works, for her to do with as she pleased, from then until our deaths. We became totally hers that lovely day.

We walked out of the church as if we were walking on air. It was so nice to be utterly poor, and better still, to know that the little we had possessed was all hers.

I had come across St. Louis Marie de Montfort several times along that journey of mine. Each time I turned away from him and from his *True Devotion*, for both strangely repelled me. It speaks of becoming a "slave" to Mary. I definitely did not like the word "slave." (So many people don't.) And I did not like his old-fashioned language, either, in French or in English.

Then again, I was busy, very busy, founding our apostolate and working among the forgotten, the despised, and the poor in the alleyways and byways of the world. I was busy trying to learn to pray, to *be* before God before *doing* for God, lest I and my spiritual children, the staff of our apostolate, should become guilty of the heresy of good works, seeking our salvation on our own strength, on our own merits, in our own good works.

My journey began long ago in my childhood. It began with my acquiring a strange love for the Holy Spirit, at an age when few pay much attention to him. It started with a nice, holy young nun who was teaching us first grade religion, and who told us about the Third Person of the Holy Trinity, drawing for us a lovely dove on the blackboard, as she spoke.

All I understood was that this dove was unloved and neglected by Catholics. So, at once, I started to pray *for* it. I continued to pray *for* the Holy Spirit until I was almost nine. Then, slowly, I understood and changed to the more orthodox way of praying *to* the Holy Spirit.

My next step was to develop a growing devotion to the hidden life of Our Lord. During the early days of Friendship House Apostolate, when I was an adult in my thirties, I learned to dwell more and more on the hidden life of Christ. It seemed as if Christ was there, hidden, for me to find.

I looked for some time for a basis on which to found my apostolic work. And slowly my heart, soul and mind turned to the hidden life of Christ and the Holy Family. That would be the answer.

It was. Like the Holy Family, we in the apostolate were poor. Like them, we would be set apart, but not made much of. Work would be our lot. Our men would work with their hands for our own needs and for those around us, as St. Joseph and Christ did. Our women would scrub, cook, and clean, even as Mary did. Here was the ideal upon which we could pattern ourselves. That is what we have tried to do ever since.

This led me to Mary. The Bogoroditza was near to my heart. I loved her greatly, turned to her always. But at this point in my life the Holy Spirit, her Spouse, led me to her in a special way.

The years went by; the journey went on. More lessons were given and learned and integrated into our works of charity. And then I met one of the de Montfort Fathers. He spoke to me of the *True Devotion*. I listened respectfully, took his book, and read it slowly.

But I laid the whole idea aside again. I did not feel any revulsion this time toward the word slave, for I had learned of the slavery of sin. It was all around me sharply delineated and outlined. But what had I to offer the gracious queen of heaven that I had not yet given away? Worldly goods? I had none. Inner detachment from them? I had been working so long on that spiritual angle that it seemed little to offer. My body? That was given over to the service of her Son long ago. My merits? How small they were! So the *True Devotion* was laid aside and gathered dust on my shelves. And the journey went on.

My son was in World War II. I had dedicated him in his infancy to Our Blessed Lady. I rededicated him, asking her to keep him safe. She did. If at all possible, my love for her grew and grew.

On August 15, 1945, which was the day World War II ended and the feast of Our Lady's Assumption, the idea of an apostolate in Combermere was conceived. Two years later

Eddie and I came to Combermere, a tiny village on the edge of nowhere, where we were to devote ourselves to the rural apostolate.

Thus, Madonna House was born, with its door painted blue in her honor. It was Mary's house and she became co-foundress of this new province of Friendship House.

In 1950, at the summer school of lay Catholic Action which we organized every year for the youth of the United States and Canada, Father John Callahan came to speak on the spiritual foundations of Catholic Action. He spoke beautifully and he brought the *True Devotion* right into the middle of it all.

Suddenly the veil was lifted and I saw a whole pattern fall into line. God the Father, to whom I had been going for so long, chose Mary to bring the Lord of Hosts to us. She was the way of his Incarnation. The Holy Spirit was her Spouse. The hidden life, which I considered the school of Christ, was also the school of Mary's love for him, for us. The Incarnation and the Redemption hung upon her yes.

To Jesus through Mary: Why, that was logical and real! That was the way to him who was himself the way, the truth, and the life.

It staggered me. Father Callahan left to return to his home diocese. I waited until Christmas and his return. I asked him many questions. He answered them all. Then Eddie and I made the three-week preparation which has been prescribed for those wishing to make the de Montfort consecration. We completed it on the feast of her Purification, a feast which now is celebrated as the feast of the Presentation of Jesus in the Temple. We consecrated ourselves to her entirely and forever. The long journey was ended. Or had it only begun?

A Poem

Years later, Catherine recalled that day in this poem written to Eddie.

The city just woke up ...
So did we.
Our hearts were full of joy
Yours and mine
Because this was the day,
The day we had chosen quite a while ago
To dedicate ourselves,
Our earthly and spiritual goods ...
In fact, all that we are and were
To Mary—the Mother of our Love.

The air was clean, the sun was shining ...
There was little snow upon the streets.
We walked, holding hands together
To that old church they call the French.

There, after Mass
Before Our Lady of the Cape
We recited together
The dedication of Louis de Montfort.

To me it wasn't his ...
It was all mine.
I knelt, it seemed
At her feet
And her mantle brushed my knees.
I was lost in joy,
And gratitude to her.

Do you remember that we knelt quite a while
In that silent, hushed church
Before her statue,
And we held hands.
Somehow our wedding rings
Suddenly became quite deep
And bound us to her in a new fashion.

We went back to the hotel.
The city was pulsating
With people ... traffic ... business ...
But we walked in sheer joy
Across the crunching snow
And yet, perhaps it wasn't the city ...
There was little snow ...
It was just simply Heaven.

A Secret

Do you want to know the secret of Mary? The first step is your consecration to Mary according to the act of Total Consecration of St. Louis de Montfort. To quote from St. Louis himself:

> A sculptor has two ways of making a statue. He may carve it out of wood, or stone, or some other suitable material. Or he may cast it in a mold. An unhappy blow of the hammer, or a slip of the chisel, or any other accident may destroy the carver's work, even before it has well begun. And, even when the process is successful, it takes much time to complete the figure.

Casting it in a mold requires but little work, little time, little expense. And, if the mold be perfect, and capable of reproducing the statue wanted, it forms the desired figure quickly, easily, and gently —provided the material used does not resist the operation.

Mary, the great and unique mold of God, was made by the Holy spirit to form the God-Man, the man-God. In this mold none of the features of the Godhead is missing. Therefore, whosoever is cast into it, and yields himself to the molding, receives all the features of Jesus Christ, our true God!

What a difference there is between a soul formed in Christ by the ordinary ways of those who, like the sculptor, trust in their own ingenuity and skill, and a soul which, without trusting itself, is molded by the Holy Spirit in the mold of Mary!

How many defects and imperfections one will show. How pure and heavenly will be the other; and how Christlike!*

If you want to know Our Lady's secret, you must enter her great silence. The door to this great silence is very small and narrow, and before you can enter you have to become small yourself. Small, humble, and simple, as a little child is small, humble, and simple. Then the door will seem big to you, and you will enter with ease.

---

* *The Secret of Mary,* St. Louis de Montfort, adapted by Eddie Doherty, Montfort Publications, Bayshore, NY, pp. 15-16.

Once you have entered, be silent yourself. Just sit down comfortably at Mary's feet and be silent with her. Let your silence have that quality of "listening recollection," that is so necessary for hearing her silence speak.

Forget the cares of the day, bend down and collect or re-collect all the pieces of yourself that the day in the market place and its heat have scattered all over the place. When you are "whole" again, and silent—reverently yet simply so, with the silence of a great love for Mary the Mother of God—she will arise and, taking you by the hand, lead you into the inner chamber of her Immaculate Heart, where all the words of her Son are still kept, as fresh and alive as when he spoke them.

Still silently, she will take each word, each familiar and dear word from this, her greatest treasure, and show it to you. In her hands each word will glow and open as a flower opens to the sun, and will reveal many a hidden or unclear meaning to you. And you will marvel that you did not see before.

Looking over the words of Christ with Mary is the first part of her great secret. The next will be her leading you through another door to her Spouse the Holy Spirit, the Crimson Dove. Gently she will lift you up into his blinding light. Then, if you lie still in her arms, as her small divine Son once did, you will begin to see life with the eyes of God. And all things will come together for you and make marvelous and holy sense, and you will lose all fears, for you will enter onto the first step of perfect love that "casts out all fear."

Sickness or health, joy or sorrow, wealth or poverty. Loneliness or the happiness of having many friends and loved ones around you. All will be accepted by you gladly, with that inner glow and joy that comes in seeing in each the most holy will of God and desiring nothing but what he desires for you.

Then you will begin to know a little more of her great secret—but not yet all of it. That will come later, if, content and at peace, you remain with her and the Holy Spirit and begin to live your life as God wishes you to.

There will come a day when Our Lady will slowly arise, and moving gracefully yet slowly, lead you in the dark afternoon to a hill on which three crosses stand. There she will ask you to look and see the price her Son paid for your soul. Be not afraid to weep that day. Weep for your sins and mine, and those of all born of woman. These will be good tears. She will mingle hers with yours.

Then the hill will vanish. So will the cross. And she will lead you into her Son's heart, the immense glowing furnace of love. You will understand how he loved you, and will love him in return, utterly, passionately, completely. You will live just for that loving, and for that burning that will kindle you and make you a flame of zeal, and you will bring him other souls who will love him as he should be loved.

God the Father will behold your love for his Son. And through Christ's heart, through understanding a little better his love and loving him back more, you will slowly come to the bosom of the Father. For this you were created.

Thus Mary, the Gate, will lead you to Jesus, the Way —and from there to the Father.

> Since Mary has formed Jesus Christ, the Head of the elect—the Head of the Church, the Mystical Body—she is qualified to form the members of that Head, all true Christians.

Does a mother form the head without the members, or the members without the head?

Whoever wishes to be a member of Jesus Christ must be formed in Mary through the grace of Christ. She possesses this grace in its fullness, so that she may bestow it fully upon her children.[**]

That is the secret of Mary, of which the first step is your total consecration, according to Montfort, to holy slavery to Mary. She desires greatly to reveal her secret. The price is simplicity, humility, smallness. It is little to give for such a treasure.

Let us arise hastily, and be about the most important business we have on this earth—our Father's business. Mary is the gate through which salvation came to us; we must walk through her to find the Triune God, and make our life a participation in their life—a holocaust of love.

Who is St. Louis Marie de Montfort?

Eddie Doherty wrote a biography of St. Louis de Montfort called Wisdom's Fool. *This is what Catherine penned about him.*

There lived on earth a man who was in love with Mary, the Mother of God. He was so in love that he could truly think of nothing else but his beloved. He was a priest, Louis Grignion de Montfort. He was a Frenchman.

There were two reasons he was so in love with Mary. First, she is the only gate that leads to Christ, her Son. St. Louis knew that we have to pass through that marvelously

---

[**] *The Secret of Mary,* p. 13.

wrought gate before we can find Christ, who is the only way to eternal life and glory in the bosom of God the Father.

The second reason he was in love with Mary, was Mary herself. For under each of her thousand titles, she is of surpassing beauty; and she holds the eyes of those who see well and deeply into the mysteries of our holy faith. To those who truly seek her out because they want to better know and love her and her Son, she slowly reveals secrets, as only a mother can. These are secrets of the way of love of her Son, and secret after secret of the way of loving him back. Finally she opens to them her Immaculate Heart, her last, most precious secret, in which they learn the ultimate lessons of sanctity, the lessons of total surrender to Love, to God.

Sanctity is love. A saint is a lover of God. All men and women were created to be saints, to love, and his kingdom of love begins here and now, but how few even try to begin loving on this earth!

Mary, Christ's mother, whose will is eternally united with his, desires, with a great desire, to bring him souls. To do this she uses St. Louis de Montfort to reveal her secrets to anyone of good will.

But note well, like many other secret treasure troves, this one is not easy to find and open. Many are the obstacles that we put in the way—worldliness, greed, and selfishness.

We must not give way to any of these. Let us arise and light the lamps of faith within our souls, and begin in earnest to open the doors leading to the beautiful secret chambers of Mary's secret! If we do, we will find happiness beyond expression, joy beyond telling, and peace that surpasses understanding. Oh, do begin now letting Mary take over your whole life, your goods, earthly and spiritual. Become a slave of Mary and a slave of Love.

The kingdom of Satan, the foe, is growing rapidly. Time is short. The devil delights in splitting persons who should be wholly Christ's, so that, divided within themselves, they turn their faces away and get lost in the mazes of the world, the flesh, and the devil.

Let us consider, just for an instance, why so many among us have mental illness, why there are so many nervous breakdowns. In some cases, it is because we are unable to bear the weight of our troubled, dark, insecure days and try to solve the unsolvable situation with the help of our own little intellects! We fail woefully. We succumb to the ills of the world, and become split against ourselves. How can our minds and bodies remain whole, when we, in a frenzy of confusion, try to do the impossible—serve mammon and God at the same time?

Turn to Mary. Study her secret as revealed by St. Louis de Montfort. Become her slave of love. Ask her to take over your life. And lo, all things will come to rest within you. Your house will be put in order. For she is the best house-keeper of souls that ever lived. And you will know, through her, the way to Christ, and step by step, will walk it easily.

Becoming Slaves

What a strange thing to do, many will say! I can love the Blessed Virgin without all that total consecration stuff. And why that outmoded and unpleasant word "slave?" The whole thing savors of some unhealthy religious emotionalism!

Maybe it does, superficially. Sure, I can save my soul without dedicating it to her, and the word slave does have a sort of unpleasant sound to our modern ears—unless I believe in and fear Satan, the prince of darkness.

Put it this way. We say easily enough and without a shudder, "He is a slave to drugs; she is a slave to drink." We know well enough what we mean. The word "enslaved" carries its own connotation, meaning utterly, completely given over to something, or in the full power of something. But we moderns have wandered so far away from "real Catholic language" that we seldom see things in their true light. Being a slave to drink, to drugs, to money, to lust—any of these means being a slave to sin.

Satan Laughs

Look at our world, where sin reigns so supreme that it is often not recognized for what it is. Satan laughs and hopes to confuse even those who were baptized as children, and in whose behalf godparents promised to renounce the works and pomps of Satan.

What is this darkness that surrounds us, our fear of nuclear war, of disintegration, this "unpeace" in which we have our daily existence? What is this desperate search for a happiness that eludes us as a will-o'-the-wisp? What is it but sin? We have forgotten the horror of sin. We do not remember that it is better to lose a life and a thousand worlds, than to commit one serious sin.

We take our sins lightly these days. We are often slaves of the devil. We are not necessarily aware of his chains as yet, for, while we live, the mercy of God is ever present to loosen their hold.

Yes, the world is enslaved to Satan, and seems to like it. But mention slavery, voluntary slavery to the Mother of God, whose obedience brought the Incarnation and the Redemption and opened the doors of paradise to us children of this world! Then everyone squirms, looks the other way, shakes their head, and speaks of emotionalism and religious mania! Isn't it strange?

Why Not With Her?

One can save one's soul without de Montfort's consecration to our Blessed Mother. Sure. It has been done. But why not with her? The road to Christ is narrow and steep. Who knows all its twists and turns better than she who walked every inch of it? She also knows all its short cuts, that woman who kept every word of his enshrined in her heart. Why do we go our way without her?

She was his first temple on earth.

She guided the steps of him who is the way.

God loves her above all creatures.

Her breast gave him life.

Her bosom held his head and face!

He called her mother.

And she called him, the ineffable God, "my Son"!

Why then, do without her? St. Louis de Montfort knew so much about her. He knew that the simplest and straightest way to Jesus was through Mary. He tells us about it. Forget the old-fashioned language of his book, *True Devotion to Mary.* Forget the word "slave." Pray for light by which to see Mary in all her splendor. And may the grace of being her slave come to you as it came to us!

You will become poor in the full sense of the word, for all you are and all you have will be hers. But then you will also be rich beyond all dreams, for you will be her child, her slave, her very own. She is the Mother of God—so you will be God's, and the heir to this whole earth and its beauties, as well as the heir to heaven's wealth and beauty, God himself.

It is all yours for the taking. I give you the freedom of the slaves of Mary. Alleluia!

Letter to a Friend

Your long letter is still on my desk. I have read it and re-read it many times. It is that kind of letter. It demands all the attention and prayer I can give it.

Yet it is not an unusual letter, in the sense that there are many, many Catholics who want to go directly to Jesus, and cannot see why they should make this urgent and vital journey, in what seems to them a roundabout way—through a creature, Mary.

At first one may indeed marshal many seemingly logical arguments for that point of view. Yours seem quite good. Yet, they all disintegrate and vanish before one cardinal fact which is manifested to us every holy season of Christmastide, and in the tremendous feast of Epiphany which it includes. This fact is that God choose to become man through Mary—and thus our redemption began in her womb!

Since God chose to come to us through her, what other way can we go to God? You may want to answer that he also said, "I am the way." But if you seek Jesus without Mary, truly you seek him in vain.

This is the acceptable time for you to arise and begin your journey inward, dear friend. It is that long, often dark, and usually strange journey any of us in search of God must undertake sooner or later, for we will find him dwelling within ourselves, within all of us who have been baptized in his name and who abide in the state of his grace.

This is a good time to start on this journey, as on the journey of the holy three wisemen toward the Epiphany, seeking Christ in Bethlehem. But before you start, go and sell all you possess, and trade it for your share of myrrh, frankincense, and gold. For without these gifts, you cannot reach the king.

Myrrh is a bittersweet herb, hard to grow to maturity. Its other name is humility. You will have to fill your hands full with it. But where shall you find it? There is truly one soil, one garden, where it grows in great profusion—Mary.

Therefore, before you start on that journey, you will have to find and cultivate Mary. There won't be much work to it. No. All you will have to do is sit at her feet, listen to her silence speak, and gather it up carefully, as it falls, drop by drop, into your cupped hands.

First you will hear the sweet silence of a young girl who has just said her immense yes to God and now feels the fruit of his love growing within her. Then, the bitter-tasting silence of the mother of all sorrows, who stands straight, unflinching, and compassionate under the cross of her dying Son and ceaselessly repeats her yes again and again, in passionate love and utter humility, with lips that mirror all the suffering and pain that ever was, is, and shall be.

See, your cupped hands now hold enough myrrh to take to the king. Only the boundless humility of the little girl and the sorrowful woman could produce such exquisite scent.

Next is frankincense. For this, you will have to search well within yourself. It is the stuff that church incense is made of and which produces the beautiful gray-blue smoke that rises up, up, up to the very throne of God, in a silent chant of love and perfume.

But where within yourself will you find the poverty, chastity, and obedience of which this frankincense is made? Alone, it is hard to find. But there is one person, a creature like you, who can show you where these dwell.

She is Mary, the mother of the holy pauper who had nowhere to lay his head except the beam of a cross; Mary who was chastity itself, a virgin mother. She is so transparent, so translucent in purity, that when you look at her, you see God; Mary, who obeyed so perfectly, so swiftly, and with such a passionate abandonment of love, all gathered up in one single word—fiat, yes, be it done!

Ask Mary, then, to show you where these virtues lie hidden in you and your hands will overflow with frankincense, and you will be able to see the king of glory.

Still, you must find gold. For it, men will go far and dig deep into the bowels of the earth. And so must you dig deep. Descend, descend into the depths of yourself, your true self. And come up with your selfish self—dead. Then you will have more gold to give the king of love than your weak hands can carry. To come before his face we must all be emptied of the self that alone can keep him from filling us. But gold, dear friend, is heavy. And to carry it on the long, long journey to the king, you must have help.

Help lies close, very close. Give up that selfish self of yours completely. If you surrender it, and all that you have and are, to Mary in a passionate total consecration of love of her and her Son, then you, their slave, will reign. And Mary will call on the principalities, powers, dominations, archangels, angels, seraphim, and cherubim to carry your gold for you.

Before you realize it, you will be kneeling before her Son our king, kneeling with hands full of gifts for the Christ child. And this, your Epiphany, will last until you die. And when you die, Mary will be there to take your soul and present it to God the Father, God the Son, God the Holy Spirit—a soul immaculate and white, as souls who belong to her in glorious slavery are.

Listen well. There is no way but through Mary to Jesus. For without Mary there would be no Christmas, no Epiphany and no magi, no kings undertaking long journeys by the guidance of the one bright star.

Without Mary, we would have no Golgotha, no Cross on it—and no Easter! Without Mary, you would not be a Catholic, nor would I. All this came to pass, all this was given to us, because a little girl almost two thousand years ago, said one single, small word—yes!

Why, then, seek elsewhere a short cut to God, when it lies so close at hand, so easy to reach? This "garden enclosed" of unsurpassed beauty is Mary. Open the gates of it, dear friend, and enter, and you will find him whom your heart seeks so passionately. He is waiting for you within those lovely gates.

Eddie Doherty wrote adapted versions of The Secret of Mary *and* True Devotion to Mary *for the de Montfort Fathers, using more contemporary language. They are in their fourth and fifth printings, and have reached thousands of hungry hearts.*

Litanies

7

Litanies

Litany of Our Lady

It is spring! All creatures praise her! Listen to the world reciting the litany of the one who played before the face of God. Austere and unchangeable, the tall pines repeat and repeat:

Holy Mary,

as they sway in the spring breezes. Gay and young, the pussy willows chant fast and joyously, as children will:

Holy Mother of God,
Holy Virgin of Virgins,
Mother of Christ,
Mother of Divine Grace,
Mother most Pure.

Daffodils take up the holy song, swaying as they chant:

Mary most Chaste,
Mother Inviolate,
Mother Undefiled,
Mother most Admirable,
Mother of Good Counsel,
Mother of Our Creator.

The green grass, new and shining, takes it up from there:

> *Virgin most Prudent,*
> *Virgin most Venerable,*
> *Virgin most Renowned,*
> *Virgin most Powerful,*
> *Virgin most Merciful,*
> *Virgin most Faithful.*

Hidden far away from the world, monks and nuns chant slowly and beautifully in half-lit chapels at the dawn of day:

> *Mirror of Justice,*
> *Seat of Wisdom,*
> *Cause of our Joy,*
> *Spiritual Vessel,*
> *Vessel of Honor,*
> *Vessel of Singular Devotion,*
> *Mystical Rose,*
> *Tower of David,*
> *House of Gold,*
> *Tower of Ivory,*
> *Ark of the Covenant.*

In brilliantly lit churches through all the lands, young and old come in on the choir. Quaking old voices, pure young ones, and all tones in between say, reverently and slowly, the titles of the woman who is clothed with the sun and has the moon under her feet:

> *Gate of Heaven,*
> *Morning Star.*

From uncounted beds of pain, the sick raise their voices, and come in beautifully on a high note:

> *Health of the Sick.*

They are joined by yet another choir, who barely raise their voices, yet can somehow be heard clearly:

Refuge of Sinners,
Comforter of the Afflicted,
Help of Christians.

Suddenly, a mighty voice, blended in the crucible of suffering, comes in to lead all the rest. It is the voice of those who are the Church of Silence, those who are persecuted, not able to speak aloud, who can be heard only by ears attuned to accents of a complete holocaust of love:

Queen of Angels,
Queen of Patriarchs,
Queen of Apostles,
Queen of Martyrs,
Queen of Confessors,
Queen of Virgins,
Queen of All Saints.

Almost the end, and yet a new voice comes in stronger, greater, more powerful than any yet raised in praise of this woman beyond all praise. Alone in his chapel, the Pope, the Vicar of Christ, sings—and gladness comes softly into the chant. Now the choir is complete. Now, indeed, the praises are lifted up unto her feet:

Queen Conceived without Original Sin,
Queen of the Most Holy Rosary,
Queen of Peace,
Queen Assumed into Heaven. Alleluia!

Litany of the Poor

Mother of the Dispossessed—come and teach us anew the luminous words of your Son. We know them by rote. But they seem to have lost much of their meaning for us children of this idolatrous age of gadgets, TVs, computers, and comforts. We are full of "self." We are too concerned with feeding, pampering, and amusing our bodies and minds.

Take each of his words, gently, Mother, and slowly open to us its depths, its beauty, and the fullness of its meaning. Then, filled with its light, we may change our ways, forget ourselves, and open our hearts and homes to the dispossessed of this world, so that we may not become the dispossessed of the next.

Mother of the Hungry—come and teach us anew the meaning of the brotherhood of men under the fatherhood of God. You who are mother of both God and man, the bridge between us, take us by the hand and show us once again the heart of your Son who died for love of us and who, not content with that, gave us the Eucharist, made himself our Food.

Come and sit at our overladen tables and tell us about all the hungry people in our cities, our country, and all the other countries of the world. Walk with us through our food-filled warehouses, and beg your Son to let us see the contrast with his eyes, lest we re-enact the scene of Lazarus and the rich young man, lest we this time play the part of the unmerciful and damned (Lk 16:19-31).

Mother of the Forgotten and Lonely—come and teach us to understand your Son's parable of the vine and its branches (Jn 15:1-8). Show us how that makes us one in him. Bring

St. Paul with you to tell us, again and again, in his ringing voice, about Christ being the head, and we the members of his Mystical Body (Col 1:15-18, 1 Cor 12:12-30).

Explain to us, then, how no one should be forgotten or lonely, since we are all one in him who lovingly never forgets. If one of the cells of the body forgets, it dies, for the bond of unity, of charity, is broken and if it is not restored in life, it will remain broken in death. Charity's other name is love. And love is God.

Mother of the Sick—come and teach us anew the meaning of your Son's words, "I was sick and you visited me." Tell us again that there are three ways of seeing, touching, and serving your Son—in the Blessed Sacrament; in deep faith in his priests, and in deep, respectful love of them; and in our neighbor, especially in our sick, forgotten, lonely, hungry, thirsty, dispossessed neighbor.

O Mother, Health of the Sick—come, come, beloved, and teach us, before it is too late, before we die of the inner sickness that seems to ail us all these strange days. Let all humanity renew its beauty and its love, as the entire earth does every spring. Do not let us die of the sickness of catering to self or of being "busy" about anything and everything but the one thing that matters—the kingdom of God, the kingdom of your Son.

Queen of Heaven and Earth, Queen of the Universe —behold us sunk in the sea of self, interested in only those things that matter least, not interested really deeply in those that matter most! Life is so short. Eternity so long. Fools that we are, we seem to have forgotten this! Show it to us anew, as only you can. Wake us up, before it is too late, so that we may live in the light of Christ's face instead of in the darkness of our own.

Your Son raised the dead to life. Please intercede for us before him, and beg him to resurrect charity in our hearts. Pray that we may show once more to a pagan world, how Christians love one another, and, by doing so, also show the face of your Son to unbelieving and wounded hearts and souls.

Mother of God, have pity on us! Come. Come now. We need you so!

Mary of the Visitation

Not Mary of the sentimental pictures. Not Mary of the many, endless, pious, pietistic stories. No.

Mary, the teenaged girl, filled with the wisdom of God and of the ages. Mary, talking to an angel with dignity and directness. Mary of the immense fiat, said with a humility that surpasses all understanding.

Mary of the Visitation. Selfless. Forgetting her own precarious position and fearlessly going to assist Elizabeth. Mary the poet, the handmaid of the Lord singing her magnificent magnificat: "My soul magnifies the Lord!"(Lk 1:46-55). Mary, the Mother of God, the poor woman of Bethlehem. Mary, the housewife in Nazareth. Mary of the hidden life. Mary under the Cross, sharing Christ's passion and Christ's love. Loving even those who crucified Him. Mary of the Pieta.

Nowhere is there anything sentimental about Mary. From the moment she entered the pages of history, she became our model. Truly, we go to Jesus through Mary. First, because he came through her to us. Then because she teaches by example all that we need so desperately to learn.

We who walk in fears, whose days are filled with neurotic anxieties, who won't believe unless we "see and touch." How desperately we need you, Mary of the Annunciation.

We who worship self so constantly that each has become a lonely island unable to communicate with another, let alone love another, how desperately we need you, Mary of the Visitation!

We who are afraid of the slightest discomfort, whose lives revolve around more cars, more bathrooms, more TVs, more gadgets, more material wealth and goods, how desperately we need you, Mary of Bethlehem and Nazareth!

We, the lonely ones always seeking a crowd, always on the go—to this meeting, that cocktail party, this dance, that date—how desperately we need you, Mary of the Hidden Life!

We who are so fearful of pain, so afraid of the Cross, so eager to be cross-less Catholics, how desperately we need you, Mary of Golgotha, Mary of the Pieta!

We who are afraid to love our own, even our friends, who have forgotten oh, so often, the very meaning of love, how desperately we need you, Mary, loving Mother of Humankind!

Mary of a thousand titles, Mary my mother, teach me, teach us, faith, trust, selflessness, poverty, detachment, obedience, and caritas, love of your Son! Amen.

Seat of Wisdom

Mary, Seat of Wisdom—Give us wisdom in this foolish and frightening age of ours, to understand your Son, to grasp that our happiness lies in knowing that he loved us first and in loving him back! Yes, him, and our neighbor as ourselves, so that we might bring peace to this war-torn world, of which the cold war was the lesser one, and the one that we wage against ourselves and our selfishness, the greater.

Mary, Cause of Our Joy—Teach us, once again, the meaning of the word joy. We who seem the most joyless generation who ever lived on this earth, and who vainly seek joy in things that are so utterly joyless!

Mary, Gate of Heaven—Teach us the way to heaven as you would little children, all over again. For we have ceased calling heaven "heaven," and call it "space," and strut around like peacocks, priding ourselves on the conquest of it.

Mary, Morning Star—Teach us to see stars again, for our eyes are blinded with neon lights, with fluorescent lights, with all kinds of lights except starlights.

Mary, Health of the Sick—Touch us with your gentle hands, for we are sick. Sick with an inner sickness that devours us. Sick with status seeking. Sick with pleasure seeking. Sick with comfort seeking.

Mary, Comfort of the Afflicted—Help us to see our own afflictions that are so deep and so searing, but even more, help us to see the afflictions of others, so that, forgetting self at long last, we might arise and go to the help of your Son in others.

Mary, Refuge of Sinners—We need you, for who of us is sinless? Give us tears to wash our sins away, so that, humble and repentant, we might begin anew to build our lives and the lives of this world in the kingdom of your Son.

Mary, Queen of Peace—Do pray for us who know not peace, for we seek it everywhere where it is not. Queen of Peace, pray for us! For you are the mother of him who alone can give us peace. Amen.

Holy Mary

Holy Mary, Mother of God,
>Pray for me, sinner chastened by rods
>of life and pain.
Pray for me, Holy Mary, Mother of God,
>Mother of Men.

Holy Mary, Mother of God
>Pray for me, on the lonely road.
>Fear walks with me.
>Darkness seems to be my only company.
>I am your child, lost in the strange byways
>and highways that encompass and confuse
>the narrow way your Son bade me to tread,
>if I want to reach his heart and his marriage bed.

Holy Mary, Mother of God, pray for me.
>Long is the way, narrow and steep.
>Your child is so tired,
>and sleep is so restful,
>so quiet and so deep.
>Yet, if I stop upon this road
>that leads to the Father, Our God,
>I know I will lose the strength to arise
>and follow the steep hills that lead to the heights.

Mother of God—what awesome words!
>How could it be that femininity enfolds Divinity?
>And yet it did!

Mother of God—yet daughter of men.
     Miracle of love and grace and mercy of the Lord.
     Mind folds its wings, faith opens its arms,
     all understanding ceases to be and the soul
     is plunged into the heart
     of the Mystery *that is!*

Mother of God—flesh hiding Light, timeless, eternal,
     entering time, lying, a seed in your holy womb,
     clothing itself with your flesh,
     God incarnated through your fiat!

Mother of God—Through his birth and death
     you became
     Mother of men. Pray for them, then,
     that they in truth may all become
     brothers of your own divine Son.

Patroness
of the Laity

8

Patroness of the Laity

Arise, shine out, O Jerusalem: for your light has
come, the glory of the Lord is rising on you.

(Is 60:1)

Yes, indeed, the glory of the Lord has risen over us, the
modern children of the eternal Jerusalem, the Church. For
two thousand years we have been enlightened. For the light
of the world has dwelt among us. But have we arisen?

The truthful answer would be no. Notwithstanding the
glory of the Lord that dwelt among us; notwithstanding the
never silent voice of the Holy Father, the watchman of the
night, God's representative on earth, calling us to awaken,
we slumber on. Yet, ours *is* the century of the laity's
awakening to its apostolicity, its participation in the royal
priesthood of Christ.

Mother of the Laity

This is also the century of Mary, the Mother of God.
Think back to when the Church was just a small group of
apostles and faithful laypeople, and Mary was still on earth.
How gently she must have encouraged the often worried and
fearful little group! How she must have prayed for them to
the Father, Son, and Holy Spirit! How they must have
found in her deep strength and an infinite consolation!

It seems that today, in a very special manner, she has resumed this mothering of little groups of lay apostles which are springing up and growing rapidly, and are yet weak and frightened and "alone" in many respects.

Notice her appearing—now here, next there. Here she weeps. There she pleads. Now she is stern, then gentle. Yet always she is addressing the laity, the faithful, asking for prayers, for sacrifices, for penance, and for works of zeal. It seems as if she is taking us under the blue mantle of her love.

There is, there must be, a connection between the spread of the apostolate of the laity and Mary's concern about our sad plight! There are arising men and women of sanctity and learning who will open the heart of this, explaining in words of love and fire the theological verities that merge the apostolate of the laity with Mary.

But even the unlearned, whose hearts are aflame with love of God, his Virgin Mother, and his beloved Church, can see, be it ever so faintly, that following the apostolate of the laity demands a life that is rooted in a reason deeply illuminated by faith directing the will toward living and integrating that faith utterly, completely, and without compromise into our everyday life—in business, home life, school, and in all the "market places" of the world.

The apostolate of the laity means walking the royal road to Christ, lightly burdened, and guided by the light of the commandments of God, the spirit of his counsels and the laws of the Church.

We all know this road is narrow, steep, lonely, and sometimes frighteningly dark to our human eyes. It is bordered on both sides by dangerous precipices and deceptive swamps and quicksands devised by the prince of darkness for our temptation and ruin.

The new lay apostles meet Mary here! For, in truth and in joy, she is the royal road to Christ! Make her your guide. At the sight of her, the woman clothed in light, all darkness disappears and the devil is powerless. "Through Mary to Jesus!" should be the battle cry of lay apostles.

How simple will the complex become under her guiding touch! How easy, complete offering of self! How rich poverty! How exquisite prayer! How light penance and mortification! How easy the hard will be.

Mary the mother of Christ is also the mother of lay Catholic Action, which is but love of God and neighbor in action. Let us love Mary much and well, and we shall love her Son, even unto death. If we do that, the restoration of the world to her Son will follow.

Our Patroness

I was blessed to attend a lay congress in Rome. While there, I was meditating on Our Lady. It occurred to me that if anyone should be a patroness of a lay congress, Mary should. Because, let's face it, she was a laywoman. Truly lay in the fullness of this term. She was the wife of a carpenter. She was the mother of a son. She was a housewife who kept house, sewed, wove. Didn't she weave the seamless robe of Christ? She must have been a good weaver. She washed her laundry at the same pool as all the other village women in Nazareth. In no way was she set apart from the run-of-the-mill secular world of her time; she belonged to it fully.

She lived with her Son, also a carpenter, for a number of years, and was supported by him. It is said that in his youth he was obedient to his parents, Joseph and Mary (Lk 2:51). He must have been obedient to her for quite a while.

What better model, what better patroness, what better helper to ordinary layfolks than Mary? Shouldn't we ask her help in turmoil, in a world filled with confusion, anxieties, and problems?

How Many Times?

Suddenly, out of nowhere, while Mary was busy about her chores, an angel spoke to her and gave her a fantastic, incredible message that she would be the mother of God, the long-awaited messiah.

She accepted this role with simple words, saying that she was ready to do God's will. We call it her fiat, which simply means "yes." But that was only one fiat of ten thousand she must have had to say. The next fiat was to be silent under Joseph's bewilderment. And after that, when she gave miraculous birth to her Child, what must have been her thoughts?

Later, she resumed the most humdrum life possible, for nothing special happened. This boy who was the messiah was just a boy, like any other boy. He ate. He slept. Then he grew, helped Joseph around the carpentry shop, learned the trade, and perhaps only once "stepped out of line," at the age of twelve, when he "disappeared" without his parents' knowing where, in Jerusalem (Lk 2:41-50).

Serenely, silently, she accepted all this. But she must have been wondering what it was all about, even as some of us today are wondering what it is all about. We wonder without her serenity, without her peace, without her love, and without her faith! How we need her love, her faith, her silence, her endlessly repeated fiat!

She was no ordinary woman, though she might have appeared to be one to the gaze of her neighbors. What courage it took to live that way! What immense faith!

Then, without warning probably, her Son left her, dropped everything and went preaching across Palestine. She may have followed. She may also have heard rumors, not all of them complimentary to him. So many accused him of so much! This must not have been her idea of a messiah! Or was it?

To Follow Him

Shouldn't she be the patroness of a laity that hears all kinds of rumors about Christ? It is said he is dead—that God is dead. It is said he is alive. It is said he wasn't God, only a prophet. It is said he is a myth.

To whom shall we, who have to listen to all this as she did, turn, if not to her? She will give us the courage to sort things out in the silence of our hearts, to grow in faith and in love, and to follow him, from afar or near, as she did.

Shouldn't we, those of us who believe, who suffer and are in anguish, anxiety and agony for his Church, follow her, and stand with her under the cross of her Son, in silence and in faith? Shouldn't we find, through her, the courage to keep believing, and to stand still while the Church, the bride of Christ, bleeds from a thousand wounds?

Shouldn't we turn to her who held her dead Son in her arms, when on all sides our ears hear the cry, "God is dead"? Shouldn't we turn to her to be able to bear the burden of that cry which tears the soul of a Christian apart?

If we do, she will lead us to his resurrection and show us the essence of a supreme, unbreakable faith.

Wasn't she the strength and the consoler of the apostles before Pentecost? This ordinary, Jewish laywoman?

The mystery of Mary is deep. Yet, if we turn to her, this woman wrapped in mystery and in silence, she will speak. The one through whom God came to us will lead us back to him. She is queen of apostles and of martyrs. The litanies of Our Lady call her many wondrous names. But I give her a very simple name: Mother of the People of God, who all should be and are called to be apostles of her Son. Because in baptism they died with him and rose with him!

This Is Her Age

Infinite and varied are the aspects of Mary that we can choose to write about. For she *is* all things to all men and women. Mother. Virgin. The all beautiful. Young. Middle-aged. Old—that is, in the sense of years. (It is said she was around sixty when she was assumed into heaven.) Housewife. Contemplative. Mother of laymen and women, mother of priests and nuns. Patroness of the modern lay apostolates, laywoman par excellence. Queen and humble maid. Facts in her case allow an endless variation on the theme, and yet centuries of writing have not even begun to tell of the height, depth, and grace of Miriam, mother of the Messiah.

Few write about her as a stumbling block, yet she is that too. Her own people, the Jews, seem unable to accept her. Protestant Christians find the cult and sea of Catholic words written about her incomprehensible. Pagans dismiss her more often than not. And our generation's atheists, humanists, and neo-pagans choose either to ridicule her or try to ignore her.

But somehow, neither can be done. She cannot be dismissed. This woman wrapped in silence, who spoke so little and who in her lifetime seemed almost a shadow deliberately effacing herself, stands immovable before our scoffing generation. One cannot go "around her." Nor in truth can one find Jesus without her. For undeniable is this one fact: he chose to come to us through her—and he still does.

As centuries pass, she seems to become more and more visible. The world is aware of her now as never before. Newspapers, reluctant as they may be, report her increasing numbers of apparitions. All races, creeds, and even the creedless, are compelled to witness a growing devotion to her.

Slowly, the young Jewish maiden so well hidden in the Temple of Jerusalem and then in the humdrum life of Nazareth is emerging as the woman clothed with the sun, the moon under her feet and a crown of stars on her head (Rv 12:1). Queen of the universe. Not only of our little planet earth, but the universe.

An awesome sight. A sight that brings unrest in hearts and places and countries where even her image is banned. Why is it banned? No authority bans what it does not fear. How right they are to fear her! For she is a challenge to all unlawful power and is indeed all powerful just because she is the Mother of God.

Nowhere is her power better understood than in the kingdom of darkness, which seems to be so successful these tragic days in overcoming much of our modern world. At the mere mention of Mary uncertainty and fear possess those who belong to darkness. And well it may be, for this is the Marian age. And she is indeed more powerful than all human armies arrayed for battle. Woe to them who oppose her!

And for the others who do not hate her but try to ignore her, or find her a stumbling block, she blots out her powers, and becomes the gentle woman of Nazareth, who walks with them on quiet feet through their nights and days, knowing that ignorance alone is responsible for their lack of love and understanding. Slowly, they will come to feel her presence. Alleluia! For them too, even if they know it not, this is the age of Mary. Yes, this is the age of Mary, and make no mistake, she will conquer again.

Mary Gives Me Ideas

There is no denying it, being consecrated to Mary gives me ideas; thousands of new ideas that come tumbling down into my mind, my soul, my heart, and fill them to overflowing until they spill all over the place; so much so that I seem to be forever wading through a flood of ideas. It gets so that I feel I have to give some of them away to others to share and enjoy with me.

Take, for instance, this idea that came to me recently. It came from nowhere. (Of course it could be it came from Mary, what doesn't?) It came ready-made. There was nothing I had to add to it myself. All of a sudden, there it was, full-grown, and I wondered why I had never thought of it before!

Our Lady and lay Catholic Action! Why, that was a natural. Wasn't she a laywoman? Of course she was. All the people living in Nazareth at the time would have testified to that in unison. She was a wife, a mother, a part in every normal way of that little village and its ordinary life.

The neighbors who used to drop in for a chat, as neighbors will everywhere, always saw her cooking, cleaning house, mending, sewing, weaving, or praying. She must have taken her laundry to the community pond, and washed it there with them all, listening to their humble chit-chat about daily news of troubles and sickness, birth and death, joy and sorrow, just as any laywoman would.

It is evident, then, that she knows what it is to be a layperson. Believe me, she does! But then again, she is also queen of priests. Now you can see the close relationship. Catholic Action is the participation of the laity in the apostolate of the hierarchy. Being queen of the hierarchy and a laywoman, she joins in her own person, both elements, and hence, should be patron of Catholic Action. Both the hierarchy and we should look to her clarification, indoctrination, and help in this great and universal apostolate of the Church. You can be sure that she has all the answers to it and, of course, is ever ready to give them to all who ask.

But what is the primary aim of Catholic Action, if not the sanctification of the individual? And who is there that can lead us to Jesus directly? Why, Mary, of course, through whom God the Father and God the Holy Spirit gave us Christ.

Yes, it is time for us to enter into the novitiate of Mary. She will teach us, as she alone can, the virtues that we must acquire if we seek personal sanctification. Has there ever been a human being who was more detached from self than Mary? Was not her whole life a fiat to God's divine will? Do you know anyone whose life was humility incarnate, abandonment personified, as was Mary's?

Of course she will teach these great virtues to anyone who comes to her, as only a loving mother can, especially when she knows that they are striving to do the will of God the Father as expressed by his Son's representatives on earth, the popes and bishops, who have been calling the laity to Catholic Action so urgently and for so long!

Take for example, trust in God, perseverance, and fortitude. Now recall her ways of practicing these eminent virtues throughout the passion of her Son, from the manger to the cross! At what better school than Mary's could anyone, especially the laity, learn these lessons? Or again, take obedience and the spirit of poverty, as well as the glowing, positive chastity that leads to that purity of heart that makes us see God and show his likeness to others. Mary is the sea of these virtues into which we can all plunge to be filled, impregnated with them. As for charity, love, from which all other virtues stem, who can teach us love better than the mother of Fair Love?

Let us, therefore, turn to her continually, but especially when we are weary, bewildered in the face of the ever-mounting tasks of our life, or when these same tasks lead us up the paths of loneliness, worry, and darkness. Then will the Queen of Apostles take us in her arms and kiss away, as mothers do, loneliness, worries, difficulties, darkness, weariness, and bewilderment, and give us some of her faith, courage, perseverance, fortitude, charity, humility, and trust in God to face the work of our life courageously and to lead souls to Christ through her.

Fiat!

9

Fiat!

This talk was given in Madonna House to those making and renewing their commitment. It is included here because it could easily be addressed to all Christians. This is what it means to follow Christ.

Mary was very young. She was an ordinary girl. As far as the world knew, she was not very important. But one day Gabriel, the angel of God came to her, with tidings of such importance that human minds reel before his words: "You are to conceive and bear a son.... The Holy Spirit will come upon you" (Lk 1:26-38). And, if you stop to think for just one minute, our minds *should* reel before an invitation like that.

In a manner of speaking, the messenger of God has brought an invitation to you too, for it is very easy to imagine that his call, "I have chosen you; you have not chosen me" to each one here present has come through an angel, even as it came to Mary. It is the invitation to each of us, men and women, to become the bride of God.

Mary also was a bride of God. But of course, she was infinitely greater, infinitely more immense than any one of us can ever be, utterly incomprehensible, and ineffable. And yet, the word bride is acceptable to her, for she was the spouse of the Holy Spirit.

An angel prostrated himself until his wings made a shimmering carpet before Our Lady, and spoke the awesome message that allowed people like you to come here centuries later, to this house dedicated to Our Lady. But the words of the angel would not have brought you here unless Mary had first said her "fiat," her "yes" to the angel. Immense as the message was, trembling as the angel delivering it, the little girl had to say "yes," "Let it be done;" her soul had to say "yes."

Isn't that what you and I have to say? Angels can tumble down and make a crown around us, and tell us in musical language conveying the echoes of God's voice that the Lord of hosts has chosen you, or me, to arise and follow him and only him. But unless each one of us, with our accents of many nations and many countries and many states and many provinces, answer him with our "yes," nothing will happen. God will stand there with empty arms ready to embrace you and me and take us for his own, even as the angel that made a shimmering carpet at Our Lady's feet could have returned with nothing but a "no" and there wouldn't be a Madonna House, or the things that are, and our redemption probably would have taken another way. We do not dwell on those strange thoughts, because the little girl said, fiat. But we stop right there and think: Mary and our vocation. The two are linked.

Every member of Madonna House has had the same grace that Mary had, in an infinitely smaller way. Every person of the apostolate has, in a manner of speaking, heard an angel speak. Each has said his or her fiat, or will say it.

Mary and the apostolate are enclosed in a little word—fiat—which means yes. Think of it! If you consider this one little word, you will understand its immensity. You will know that all that we are trying to teach you, and all that is being taught to us all, can be encompassed in this fiat, for the only reason for a fiat is caritas—love. And the fruit of fiat and caritas is pax—peace.

Mary and the apostolate. So simple, so clear, so easy to understand. When you really get down to hard brass tacks, you can throw out all your books if you know how to love.

She and our apostolate are one. She became the mother of the apostolate the moment she pronounced the word fiat, and a blinding light that even the angel could not look upon descended upon her and the Holy Spirit overshadowed her and she conceived the Son of God.

In another way, the same happens to each one of us. The Holy Spirit overshadows us with his graces, and with his help we each shall die to self, and have an Advent, a time of waiting, of spiritual pregnancy with Christ.

Each of us exists, even as Mary did, to give birth to Christ in us. She was full of grace. We will be full of grace too. (Not in the manner that she was, without stain of original sin; nevertheless, we will be.) She will help us to die to self, so that when we, who began our apostolate with a fiat, die and finish our apostolate, we will be able to say with the ringing voice of St. Paul, "I live not, Christ lives in me."

But let me continue the story of the annunciation. When Our Lady heard the voice of the angel, she found out that she was needed by her cousin Elizabeth and went to help her. Oh, how the annunciation blends with our apostolate, and how the visitation completes it! For what have you said your yes to? In the moment of your greatest joy or sorrow, at any moment of your life, consider. Mary left Joseph; she went. A strange mystery, is it not? She would return to him visibly pregnant. She walked away enveloped in silence. She returned in silence. She let God speak. She went on an errand of mercy.

In our apostolate, we spend our life on errands of mercy, so walk always invoking Our Lady of the Visitation.

Every step you take is for others. So naturally, Our Lady of the Visitation is right at your side. Alone, young, she traveled across dangerous country. In those days, robbers were known to be there. It wasn't an easy road. Is your road going to be easy? You're going to travel in dangerous country, very dangerous country—the country of temptations and doubts and dark nights and dryness. But you won't mind, because you will remember a frail little Jewish girl, sitting on a donkey, alone, going forth in the silence of God, the Triune God, Father, Son, and Holy Spirit, the God who dwells in your soul because she said her fiat.

You see how interwoven, living almost the same life, always together, are Mary and the apostolate. And what is your task in life? What is the work that you are going to do? Like the fruit of your being, are all the things we have just spoken about.

You will find your Bethlehem, each one of you. There will come a day in your life when you really will give birth to Christ, in the stable of Arizona, in the desert of Africa, in the snows of Canada, wherever your visitation will lead you. There, you shall give birth to Christ for all to see. Just as Our Lady of the Universe gives her Child to the world, so will you give the fruit of your growth in the Spirit, Christ, the Lord—a baby at first.

Mary will be there. She is always there at the birth of her Son in people's hearts. She is the midwife and the mother of this delicate and beautiful meeting of her Spouse, the Holy Spirit, and a human soul.

Then you will know the hidden years of Nazareth within your soul. You will know them blending together, covering time and space, because these things do not historically or even poetically follow one after another. The spiritual life is a mixture of all things at once: the joyful, the sorrowful, and the glorious mysteries. So you will know the whole life of a woman with two men, Jesus and Joseph, and in Jesus, with God.

And so you weave a sort of pattern out of your life, now going to Bethlehem, now to Nazareth. Mary will lead you to the little village of Nazareth and it will be a hidden village. She has the keys to all doors in heaven and on earth, and she will open the path for you and take you in.

Mary will take you into a house where she dwelt for thirty years with God and Joseph. And you will dwell in that house likewise. It will be a hidden house. People will not understand whom you represent and why you are there. There will be need for flights to Egypt; there will be persecution; there will be lies told about you.

Suddenly, one day, you will find yourself side-by-side with Mary in the passion of Christ; next you will return just as suddenly to Nazareth. For we are weak and small, and Our Lady gently shows us the secrets that we must know so as to reach her Son and become one with him.

We can put all this another way. The relationship between Mary and the apostolate is very simple. It's a school of love, where the Mother of Fair Love will teach you, and when you are in doubt, will comfort you. And when you are in the dark night of the soul, she will sing her lullabies to you. And across the darkness when all is aridity, when her Son seems to have disappeared, her soft voice will suddenly come to you. Who knows, will she sing in Aramaic, in

Hebrew, or in your own tongue? It matters not. Her voice is like oil on a wounded heart. No matter how dark the night, there will be light, because Mary will be there.

Mary permeates the apostolate, and you will grow in the school of love, in the hiddenness of Nazareth, in the strange flashbacks so to speak, of the flight into Egypt, and in the public life and passion of Christ. For such is the school of love; Our Lord gently grows in you. He does not immediately make himself immense and big. He knows it might break us. And before you know it, Our Lady one day will come to you and say, "Now is the time to really meet my Son in you. Behold, he is a man. Come, you who are his bride. The first part of the wedding feast is at hand." And eagerly, you shall arise and you shall go.

It is Mary who is going to lead you to the Hill of the Skull to die, finally, on the cross with Christ, so that with St. Paul you might say indeed, "I live not. Christ lives in me." Yes, this is the first part of the wedding feast.

Slowly, she will walk with you through the public life of Our Lord and will open its secrets to you. Grace will flow through her gentle hands and fall on the book that her Spouse will write for you, and all will become simple, because fundamentally, it will be the book of love. All things are simple to those who love.

And as you go through this, you will notice, finally, that she has spoken very little, that you have learned at the knees and feet of her silence, that it has enveloped you with a mantle fragrant and sweet. And whenever her silence has touched you, it has healed, and made you whole. And you will learn to be silent, silent with a depth of silence that alone allows others to hear the voice of God in you.

So, gently and slowly, you will walk with her, all of you here, and everyone else to come, unto the end of time. You will walk with her through the whole life of her Son, step by step, day by day, hour by hour, for she alone can lead you.

There, in that school of love, you will learn how to restore this world to God through her. You will know that the restoration lies not in what you *do* but in what you *are*. And you will understand that you must be nothing, nothing but a sheet of flame as a backdrop to God. Christ-bearers, life-bearers, lovers, that's all. The rest shall be added to you. She will see to it that it will.

Finally, you will arise, and from afar you will hear the sounds that will make your soul shrink and your body turn away, the sound of leather against human flesh. And you will step behind Our Lady and try to run away, and she will look at you and say, (except perhaps for when she sang you lullabies, this may be only the first or second or third time that you hear her voice) "Come, child, this is the first part of your wedding feast," and her voice will give you strength. Gently she will walk ahead and show you her flagellated Son. You will see him laden with the cross, and only because she is there will you be there. Now the silence will have a new quality, the silence of Our Lady, the Mother of Sorrows, Queen of Martyrs. You will hold on to her robes. You will tremble before the sight. But then you will witness her meeting her Son, and she will permit you to catch the glance that passes between her and him. And you will know courage and fortitude to its very depths. Then you will understand that one dies for the Beloved.

Now your step will be springy, and you will walk fast. And Our Lady will smile and step aside and let you run. Do you hear? They are nailing him. You can hear the hammer against the nails, and at times the hammer slips and hits flesh. You now have to be there. Now you know, because you saw what love is like. Now you come up and tear away your garments of self, of everything that's left that isn't God. You run towards those who nail him and you say, "Oh, Mr. Executioner," as Saint Agnes did, "See, there is an empty space on that cross, and he is my tremendous lover. I want to hang on the other side." And they will laugh and jeer at you and think it's lots of fun to look at two crucified people instead of one. And they will nail you there.

And as you will look down, the face of the Mother of God will look up and she will smile. And you will know joy beyond compare.

Mary *is* the apostolate. Remember that. Follow her. Follow her silence. Go to the school of love. Go to the woman who gave birth to perfect Love that casts our fear. Go to the Mother of God, the beloved of the Trinity, the mother of all women and men, the queen of sorrows and of martyrs. Go to find Our Lady of joy. For that is the apostolate. "I live not, Christ lives in me," and because of it I know perfect joy.

Desert Flowers

10

Desert Flowers

Compassion

Every week I spend a day in my *poustinia*, a little hut in the woods where I can be quiet, pray, and listen to God.

Often he gives me a word. The word he gave me to share with you this time is "compassion." But in my mind, or is it my heart, it is spelled "com-passion."

I sat very quietly contemplating this word. There are moments in the poustinia when an intense stillness surrounds me and it is in this stillness that the word or thought that comes to me flowers.

Still, I wondered, what did it mean? Where was it going to lead me? It was leading me to Mary: I was "Mary-bound." So I examined the word while I moved toward her. Yes, it was com-passion, meaning to share a passion, to share a pain. To be part of the pain, part of the passion, totally or partially, as the case may be. When I finally came to Mary, I rested at her feet and looked at her, and I realized suddenly and fully what this word *com-passion*, or simply *compassion*, meant— it meant Mary.

Mary was conceived without the taint of original sin. That didn't mean that she didn't have a free choice between good and evil throughout her life. She did have that free choice, otherwise her fiat—the one she said to the angel—

would not have been the freewill offering it was. I realized that her life with Jesus, which was freely embraced, was not easy. She did not always understand what many of the events of his life meant.

What did his reply to her in the temple mean when he was a boy, "Did you not know I must be about my Father's affairs?" (Lk 2:49). Or when she went to visit him and he asked, "Who are my mother and my brothers?" (Mt 12:46-50). No, she didn't understand, but she kept all his words in her heart, for she loved him intensely and he was her life.

She was the still one, the quiet one, the recollected one. She didn't speak much, for she was also the listening one; that is why she could keep so many of his words in her heart.

The still ones, the listening ones, are the children of the Father and do his will. Mary was the mother of the Son, the daughter of the Father, and the spouse of the Holy Spirit. Yes, she was the listening, praying, still one above all others. She was also the free one, and, therefore, pure of heart, and saw God. Yes, Mary quite definitely must have seen God—in many ways. Often, as in a glass, darkly. Perhaps, occasionally, in a blinding revelation of love. But that is speculation. What isn't speculation is that she followed Christ in his passion.

When I considered Christ's passion, it came to me again and again as a sort of double-header. For what is passion? Passion holds hands with love. Passion makes love sparkle and shine, leading it to the slender tops of immense mountains that lie in human hearts and can only be scaled by passionate lovers. Its roots are love. Its growth is love. Christ loved us passionately and some of us love him back passionately. Passion usually means pain. There is nothing strange about that, for love and passion not only hold hands, not only scale the top of slender mountains, but are entwined one around the other, for there is no love without pain and no pain without love. One without the other is inconceivable: love without pain is inconceivable.

Into this image of the marriage of love and passion, which the Lord accepted and through which he redeemed us, Mary suddenly enters. Mary. Pure of heart, she sees God. She followed him, her Son, right to the foot of the cross and beyond it to his grave. Hers is true "com-passion." She shares his passion, not in a physical way only but certainly in a spiritual, emotional, and deeply tragic way.

As I sat at her feet and watched her in spirit, I realized that a second fantastic question was presented to her. The first announcement of the angel who told her that she was full of grace and that God would be born of her, took faith to accept. Mary had that faith, and of her own free will accepted the invitation to be the mother of the messiah. The second question came when she heard her own Son say, from the height of his cross, "Woman, behold your son!" and to John, "Behold, your mother" (Jn 19:26-27).Once more, she was asked to do the impossible, or almost the impossible. For her Son who came to do the will of his Father was offering Mary this will of his Father. He told her at that moment that she was chosen to be the mother of mankind through St. John, and that her "com-passion" would be constantly exercised throughout the centuries, even as the mercy of God was going to be exercised throughout the centuries, for she would have to forgive the present murderers of her Son and the new murderers who would arise with every generation. Our Lady's compassion had to bear fruit—the fruit of forgiveness. And it had to do more. Through forgiveness, it had to heal all humankind. Once more the role of Mary was clarified for me.

I remembered that many people had asked me what compassion is and felt ready now to tell them. It is Mary, who experienced the passion of her Son as no one else experienced it. She truly had compassion, for she shared the passion of her Son. She shared his passionate love for humanity and for each man and woman, and she shared his pain!

Love and pain. These two words name the chalice the Father had given him to drink for all humanity and now he had forgiven them. Forgiveness too is the fruit of love, and the incredible love of God is filled with forgiveness. This chalice was given to Mary, for Jesus Christ passed through Mary, became a man with her flesh and blood, and, as such, was crucified.

Somehow, in this incredible mystery of God's dealings with mankind, a woman was asked to share the love, the pain, the forgiveness, and the healing which her Son achieved on the cross.

Because Mary accepted this role, if role it be, she became the mother of humanity, and we cannot walk through life without her, the gentle one, the compassionate one, the listening one. She is a woman who will teach us forgiveness, because she forgave unto her very depths, unto her very heights, widths, and breadths. She forgave with the forgiveness of her Son. This will heal us, for no one can heal as truly as this woman can.

The Flower of Forgiveness

I want to enter a little more deeply into the heart of Mary and talk about what her forgiveness was in its totality and in its tremendous love. Only love can forgive.

It is almost like an abyss, this forgiveness of Mary. Consider what it meant for her to forgive those who crucified her Son, who was also the Son of God. I guess she was the only person who could have done it—that is why she was so full of grace.

She is also called Queen of Martyrs. She certainly was martyred emotionally by the sight of her Son on the cross. Queen of Martyrs. We always say martyrdom hurts, and it does. When we were young some of us read the stories of the saints and dreams of glory surrounded us. We dreamed of being saints; we dreamed of going into distant lands; we dreamed of being martyred for the faith. Mary, the queen of martyrs, didn't go anywhere. She never left Palestine. She wasn't physically martyred. Nobody laid a finger on her. The Romans left her alone and the Jews didn't bother her. So why do they call her, queen of martyrs?

At this point I had to go into my heart and slowly and prayerfully ponder what forgiveness is. To forgive, totally and completely with my whole heart, my whole reason, is to obey God's commands. Greater love has no man than he who lays down his life for his friend. So martyrdom and forgiveness, in a sense, go together. One cannot say which comes first. Sometimes it takes martyrdom of the spirit, of the emotions, to consent to forgive.

Think of all the Jews who passed through the Nazi holocaust. Six million of them. Not all forgave, but I met some who did. They passed through a great martyrdom before they were able to stand before their God and say, "I forgive."

We believe in Jesus Christ, who was a Jew and who was crucified by the Romans. We too must enter that strange and arid land of martyrdom, where forgiveness dwells like a strange desert flower.

I have a little experience with this sort of thing. Many of my people were killed by the Communists. So I was confronted by the words of Christ, "Greater love has no man than he who lays down his life for his fellow man." When I left Russia I was not open to martyrdom, and yet my heart fought a strange and incredible fight. Archbishop Neil McNeil, who was the founding bishop of our Friendship House apostolate, asked me to survey the Communists in Toronto in the 1930s. I did that survey and I remember the moment when I forgave. I was visiting a Communist hall and I was listening to a lecture. A woman next to me was embroidering something and suddenly she threw it on my lap and said, "Comrade, isn't it a beautiful flag?" It was a red flag with the white hammer and sickle. I fainted.

Everything, everything in me that was of hate passed before my eyes when she threw that flag over me. When I came to, I went outside for some fresh air. On the doorsteps of a Communist hall, sitting and imbibing a little fresh air, I asked myself if I was a Christian. Because unless I forgave the red flag and what it stood for, I hadn't come anywhere near our Lady, Our Lord, the Father, Son, and Holy Spirit. I couldn't call myself a Christian. I was a hypocrite, holding somewhere deep in the recess of my heart a closed door, and behind that closed door a bunch of serpents were writhing with hate toward my fellow human beings. So I *had* to forgive.

Mary was called queen of martyrs, without ever having been martyred. She was born full of grace without stain of original sin. The fact was that she was in love with God. She said, "Be it done unto me according to your will." She allowed his will to be done in her.

Hundreds of people pass through Madonna House and ask, "What is God's will?" Wait and see, but while you wait, pray. That, quite evidently, is what Mary did, from the day of her presentation in the temple and probably from her birthday. She was the Queen of the Martyrs. She calls all of us in every generation, in every decade, to experience that martyrdom that she has experienced. Some spiritual writers call it "white martyrdom," as distinguished from a bloody one. Mary, Queen of Martyrs. Each one of us can say to her, "Help me not to dislike anyone, not to hate anyone, not to fear anyone, because fear is like an immense wall that separates people."

Mary, Queen of Martyrs, we dimly understand how you found forgiveness for all of us while your crucified Son was lying on your lap. He is in our heart. Mary, Queen of Martyrs, give us courage to go deep into the desert to be able to pluck the flower of forgiveness.

The Effacement of Our Lady

I've been mediating quite a bit on the effacement of Mary. If you really scan the Gospels, and even the Old Testament where some predictions about her are written, you find a sort of strange silence. Luke talks about her in the story of the birth of Christ, and what she said to the angel; but after that not much. She walks through the gospel in almost complete silence. She accepts things.

I think of the three recorded situations where she accepted things.

Once, when Christ was twelve years old and teaching the people in the synagogue, she and St. Joseph searched all over for him and on finding him, she gently rebuked him.

He said to her, "Don't you know that I'm about my Father's business?" (Lk 2:49).

Secondly, the apostles came to Jesus and said, "Your mother is outside. She wants to see you." He turned around and looked at the crowd and said, (in a sense), "I have no mother. You are my mothers and brothers and sisters" (Mt 12:46-50), calling to the laity, looking to all of us.

What she went through during his passion, we don't know. Jesus said to St. John, "Take this woman and look after her" (Jn 19:27). We don't hear any answer from her. In each of these situations, there is some kind of effacement.

In Russian icons Mary is always seen with Christ as a child. She is presenting the Child to the world. One of the de Montfort fathers went to Russia. He told me how deeply the Russians incorporate the Virgin into their lives. They have done so with a totality that is incredible to the West. The Akathist hymn to Our Lady (the Office of Praise to her), for instance, is something that everybody in Russia recites. In Russia we learned at an early age, and I think you do too, that Our Lady effaces herself before her Son, presenting him to the world, so you naturally go through Mary to her Son. She is like a door, and it's important to think of her that way. She is a door to bring people's hearts to her Child.

What does this strange effacement, this strange taking of second place mean? It is as if she were hiding somewhere in the background and it takes effort to remember her. What has this got to do with us? Well, I'll ask you point blank, brutally: How well are we effacing ourselves to allow Christ to come forth from us? I confess that after many years of praying and loving God and my neighbor, I still need more effacement, some more of that strange ability that she had and which is mine and yours for the asking, to always present the Child to others.

But we're so preoccupied with ourselves. If you listen to people talk, what is the pronoun you hear all the time? Isn't it the pronoun "I"? You get the picture? It isn't a pretty, nice picture but it's a true one. We put ourselves always ahead of everything, even God. Actually, we would like God to do our will instead of our having to do his will. If we could only manipulate God! But try as we may, we can't manipulate him.

Anyhow, people say, "I want to know the will of God." I feel like looking into their eyes and saying, "Do you?" Because there are certainly moments in my life when the last thing I want to do is the will of God, and I would be a hypocrite if I said, "All I want to do is the will of God." I live on an island apart from the main house of Madonna House and some days I don't want to cross the bridge to come over to the main house. I don't want to face a lot of people on certain days—and I talk about loving people! I do love them, but they get in my hair, and I'm human, and so I don't feel like it. But the point is that I disregard my feelings and I proceed across the bridge and once I'm on the other side, I'm in love with everybody again. (Periodically, there are moments when I'm not in love even after I cross the bridge, *but then I pray.* That is the only thing I can do.) We must meditate on walking in the footsteps of Our Lady in the ordinary things of life.

A Crown

I was thinking about the custom we used to have of crowning Our Lady during her month of May. Today we need to re-establish this simple custom, but our crowning should be somewhat different.

Consider who Mary was—a simple woman, a housewife. She was a woman who carried her laundry to the pool and washed it there with all her neighbors, listening to whatever anyone wanted to tell her.

She is the same today. She is the listening one, because she is the silent one. She is the one we should turn to when our loneliness, begotten by our tragic technological society, brings us to the borderline of despair.

Mary is the quiet one who now, as then, can bring peace to those she listens to.

Mary is a poor woman who moves among all the poor of the world as one of us, who understands us and whom we understand. Who of us isn't poor? What about that millionaire who has nothing but his money? He needs to go to Mary, the woman who was poor. She still is.

In our age, so many young people are desperately seeking a mother, for so many mothers are not there for their children. Mary is there, for she is the mother of humanity. She is the one who will console and understand and take youth by the hand and lead them to her Son, whom they are seeking so constantly, so endlessly.

Yes, May was the time when we crowned Our Lady with a flower crown, making her, as it were, queen of heaven, which she must be. But today we must crown her with our love. We must bring to her a crown of our needs, our loneliness, our poverty, and our seeking of her Son. It will be a crown composed of so many, many pieces, which she alone can put together; and which she will not keep but hand back to us with a gesture of love, compassion, and tenderness.

Eternal Spring of Hope

Again, my prayer turns to Mary who, from the moment of her fiat, became the eternal spring of hope.

Hope? How much of it is left in the world? It seems to have died in Hiroshima, or was it in Vietnam? Or was it buried in a coffin-like signature of the judges of the Supreme Court of the United States when they signed their decision to allow abortion?

"A cry was heard in Ramah"; perhaps it was more muted than in Palestine at the slaughter of the innocents (Mt 2:16-18), but it was a keening over hope.

It is spring, the time for all things to be renewed, from the little blade of grass to the green leaves of the immense oak tree. Alone, human efforts appear to be hopeless. There is so much violence across this planet earth! So much greed, selfishness, arrogance, and pride seem to stalk our hearts, that hope is trampled under our feet. But there is God. And there is Mary, the mother of our hope, for she is the Mother of God. Mary, who was dedicated to God at the temple in her youth, is herself the most precious temple of all. She learned to pray and today she teaches us how to pray!

We are beginning to pray. Across this whole earth of ours, one can hear prayer. The prayer of faith, of love, and of hope is raised in songs and alleluias. The soft whispering of prayer has people across the world speaking to God face to face, and there is the intense prayer that cannot be heard, the prayer of those who have transcended words and pray silently to the gentle, listening God.

Slowly, if the prayer continues, we will begin to see ourselves as we are, and seeing ourselves as we are, we will begin, in hope, to change our violent ways and become loving and forgiving.

Slowly, as we speak and listen to God, he will open to us many new ways that will stop the keening of women over their children, and the laughter of children will ring out again across the earth. As we continue to pray, the fire of the bomb will die, nuclear weapons will be silenced, and the fire of love will grow slowly, bringing all of us to the brotherhood of man under the fatherhood of God.

It is spring in the month of Mary, the month of hope that cannot die.

Our Lady of Silence

Our Lady of Silence is a title under which Mary is well known and much beloved in Russia, my native land. I met her that way early in my childhood. Children's tales and those of holy pilgrims first brought her to me and taught me that her silence was so full of beauty and song that if only people took time to listen to it, they would have enough of both to last into eternity.

Later, I learned that if anyone wants to find their way to Christ the Lord, they have to enter the school of Our Lady's silence, for she is the gate to Christ, who is the way to the bosom of the Father, and her silence teaches all the short cuts to the way.

Later again, I came to know the healing powers of her silence and came to rest in it when the wounds and weariness of life made me almost lifeless. For her silence, fragrant and filled with the sweet smell of unknown heavenly perfume, was like oil to my wounds and wine to my weariness.

One day I discovered that when I dwelt in her silence a while, she who gave us the incarnate Lord of Hosts would also share it with me. I followed in her footsteps with ease and joy. She led me through the life of her Son, the Desired One, from the annunciation of his birth to his ascension into heaven. I saw it all through her eyes and drew slowly unto the Triune God of whom she was the daughter, mother and spouse.

Yet knowing all this, there was a time when I stayed outside her silence. I seemed to have lost or forgotten the small narrow door to it, so well hidden in her, as in a garden enclosed. This happened when I came to North America —into a vast, glorious land where few knew her under the title of Silence and where everyone lived amid noise—the noise of a million wondrous machines. The machines made life easier for them, except for one thing—the noise deafened them. It was a noise from which they sought escape in other noises, mostly the noise of speech. I grew quite weary at times, so weary that I, too, was too tired to seek her in her holy healing silence!

Then one day I met a youth who had come to spend some time to study the lay apostolate, Madonna House style. There was about him a peace that I was first hard put to understand until one day he came to say goodbye. He was leaving for a Trappist Monastery. A Trappist Monastery! The two words were like a key placed in my hands! Though I knew of such monasteries, I had forgotten them! But now even the thought of them brought back pools of healing silence, each reflecting the face of Our Lady of Silence, and set my feet running back to her!

Yet, somehow the way was long and I again grew weary. Again the voice of her silence called me gently, this time through books written by Trappists who, though they wrote words, wrote them between the lines of the holy silence— hers—that they dwelt in. Like the perfume of costly ointments the echoes of her silence drew me closer and closer. And I was not the only one; three more young people arose to go forth to the Trappists and become dwellers in her silence.

Then she sent me one returning from there after six years of being in the very heart of it. He was sick, quite sick, but, oh, how he healed all those he touched, because he shared her silence with all of us! I remember walking with him from church along a road flanked with dark pines that seemed as sentinels guarding some unseen treasure. He walked in a silence that softly sang a continuous song of love. One day I received a well wrapped package from one of the monasteries of La Trappe, and when I opened it, there she was—Our Lady of Silence! It was a picture painted by a Trappist monk, one of the few pictures saved from a fire in one of their monasteries. She was sent to thank me, the note said, for taking care of their sick son.

She dwells with me today, Our Lady of Silence, the lady whom I had known from early years and lost awhile in the beautiful land of noisy machines. A vigil light burns before her, night and day. My special intention book, where I write the names of those who ask my poor prayers, stands next to her. For I have a strange, childlike idea that during the silent hours of the night she breaks her silence to read the intentions to her Son.

Yes, Our Lady of La Trappe, Our Lady of Silence dwells with us. And I have found once more the narrow, little door that leads to her, the garden enclosed, and opened it with the keys given me by one of her Trappist sons.

Simplicity

11

Simplicity

*In the later years of her life, Catherine had a burning
desire to write a book on Our Lady, a book that would speak
of her ordinary life. Such a book, she felt, was needed to
bring Our Lady into the center of our lives. Before Catherine
could complete her dream, she entered into her last illness. In
this chapter are compiled from her last dictations and other
recent sources the thoughts that were most on her heart. She
had a favorite prayer: "Give me the heart of a child, and the
awesome courage to live it out." In her last years she wrote
with the heart of a child, and did live it out with awesome
courage. To understand what she wrote we must enter into an
intimacy, perhaps unfamiliar to many of us, with the Mother
of God. It is the fruit of a lifetime lived in the heart of the
Trinity and of Our Lady in the center of the Holy Family.
Only the heart of a child will comprehend.*

As She Really Is

Consider Mary as she really is. Everybody glorifies her.
Of course she is to be glorified. She is the Mother of God. I
have read many books about Our Lady praising her. I have
read many books by theologians telling me who and what
she is and what she has done. But there are many women
like myself who feel that she is so high up that nobody can

touch her. And this isn't true. It is true that she's high up, but she's also very ordinary. She washed and scrubbed and cleaned. So I would like to tell of her ordinary life.

What did she do all day? What would she do if she were writing a column "My Day" as Eleanor Roosevelt did? What would "My Day" by Our Lady be like?

I imagine it to be a very simple ordinary day. She was married to a carpenter. She wasn't a big shot in Nazareth. Nazareth was a small town. Joseph wasn't a big shot. She tended to her husband and Son, especially when her Son was small. She cooked, she scrubbed, she washed and wove and attended to the garden and did the laundry. I revel in her normality, because she is ordinary and at the same time extraordinary.

Nobody knew that there was anything special about her, except perhaps her pregnancy, but that was past. It was an ordinary household, and that is a most fantastic thing. Our Lord chose a working woman for his mother! A working woman! Somehow or other, this stuns me. I marvel at all the things that happened to her without anything seeming to happen.

It is marvelous, the ordinariness of Our Lady. It is a miracle. Our Lady is the first person who really knew how to do the will of God in its minute details.

You Asked Me

You asked me to explain who Our Lady is. It is almost impossible, but I will try. You could say that she's the gate—the gate to the way to the Father, because it is through her that Christ came to us and it is through her that we return to him.

Every Russian understands that without any special devotions. How important she is in our life is difficult to express. We think of her in two terms; as an ordinary, young girl who was a teenager when she became pregnant and the mature woman strong enough to stand silent and surrendering under the cross of her Son.

There is a legend that says that two learned rabbis were discussing the Scriptures about the coming messiah, and a very humble, little girl from Nazareth made obeisance to them when passing by. It was Mary. They didn't notice her. That happens to us sometimes.

She is the very fabric of our lives. Her fiat is our fiat. But we are not stupid enough to think that she only said one fiat. She said thousands. We know that instinctively, because she didn't understand, she believed. "Let it be done to me according to your Word. Lord, speak, your servant is listening."

When she became pregnant, it was a great shame because she and Joseph were not married yet, only betrothed, and he was going to put her away. Never once did she open her mouth to justify herself. Now, she was not Christ before Pilate. She was an ordinary girl from a little village. Doesn't that give us courage to be silent before unjust accusations? She didn't think it out theologically. She's so simple.

She's a mother and she attracts all mothers. She's a virgin and she attracts the young. She attracts old maids. She got up in the morning, and on some days of the week carried the laundry to the pool. The women of Nazareth must have come to her constantly because she was who she was. She must have kept, not a cookie jar, but the Eastern sweets that Eastern people love, and children must have come to her.

We think of her in realistic terms, but secondly, we also we think of her as the woman with the power to stand silently under the cross of her Son, and in some incredible way, realize at that moment that she was chosen to be the mother of all the men and women for whom he had died.

She's the woman of speech and the woman of silence. She's stronger than an army in battle array and as weak as only a woman can be with God. She dusted and she cleaned. She cooked and she knew how to weave. Her life was a sea of small things—so insignificantly small that they're almost not worth mentioning. The corn had to be ground, her house swept, the meals prepared; day after day, the Mother of God did those things.

From her we can learn the quality of listening, and of taking up human words as well as God's words, holding them in our hearts until the Holy Spirit cracks them wide open and gives the answer to us as he did to her.

We Russians have no special devotion to Our Lady because she's just as much a part and parcel of our life as breathing. It's impossible to have devotion to breathing! I don't have any devotion to taking air in and letting it out —it's my life. If I stop breathing, I die. That's the way it is.

Perhaps I don't say enough about Our Lady in her house, Madonna House. If you don't know her, you will never know her Son, because the immense mystery of our faith is that God chose this ordinary village girl for his mother. Do you get the picture? The immense and infinite God bent low to a teenaged girl and asked her if she wanted to be the mother of his Son. "How will it happen, for I know no man?" she asked. The answer came, "The Holy Spirit will overshadow you." She said this "yes," and then a thousand, million "yeses," the ones that we refuse to say.

Jesus lived with her for a long time after Joseph died. He was the bread-winner. He made chairs and tables. He was a man. And then one day, without saying much to her, he went away. And a strange mystery began: with the holy women, she evidently followed him, but she still had the house in Nazareth. And what did she hear him say? What did she hear other people say? She heard many things and most of them were not complimentary to him. When he returned to his own home they wanted to chase him out and stone him, but he disappeared. How did she feel? Those people were their neighbors. We do not know and cannot tell. (How do we react to situations that are somewhat like these? Somebody insults our relatives, or our friends, or our work. What's our reaction?)

Then he became a preacher, a worker of miracles. Who knows what miracles she was present at? She didn't say. But, one day she went to see him, and the people said, "Your mother is outside." He said, "Who is my mother?" And again, she must have made a strange "fiat," perhaps without understanding. What was it like, day in and day out, being the mother of this strange man, in the surroundings that she was brought up in and lived in—the culture, the religion of an obedient daughter of Israel? How did she feel about that strange Son of hers? Her days must have been filled with little "fiats" and big "fiats."

Later she was there when he was flagellated. She followed him to his passion. We have no record that she wept. We have no record that she spoke. We have only a record that she went to live with John the Beloved. And we have a sense, if we read the Scripture, that after his death, and even after his resurrection, the eleven frightened apostles went into an upper room somewhere and stayed there as he told them. She was there too, and she seemed to be the mainstay of those men, who only the day before, perhaps, didn't notice her when she was following him with the other three women.

Who is Our Lady? A woman like you and me. Why did God choose her to be his mother? Why did she become the gate?

It's difficult to speak of your breath. It is difficult to speak of someone whom I consider to be the real mother of Madonna House. She is someone to whom my heart goes out all day and who is with me as a friend, and with whom I can talk. We all should talk to her about her Son. For you see, she changed his diapers and he drank her milk, and she kissed his hurts away as any woman does to her toddler. He scratched himself, so she kissed it away. He fell and he got up and he grew up, and she probably said, "Eat your porridge," and "Don't forget your sandals. It's wet."

Who else has lived with God as Mary has? To whom else can we go and find out that he is really a man? From whom shall we know the Incarnate One better than from the woman who carried him for nine months in her womb?

How can anyone talk about throwing out devotions to Our Lady? Do you want to throw out the woman who was pregnant with God and who will lead you always to him?

It is not astonishing that you know little about her, if you think of her mainly as Queen of the Angels or Queen of the Universe. For you see, God was a carpenter and she was a housewife. And God is in heaven and he still has calloused hands in his glorified body. And she, who also has been assumed into heaven and has a glorified body, still has hands that show she was just a working woman, that she was a girl like you. They say she lived to be about sixty, so she must have been a woman like me. She is all things to all of us because she is the mother of mankind.

We are catching sight of a mystery encased in human flesh, born from a human mother and a human father, Joachim and Anne. She was begotten by two people just as you and I were each begotten by two people. She was just an ordinary human creature.

How can you not love her? How can you not go to her, run to her? She has the secret of everything, now that she is where she is. And when you worry about some kind of a mystery or have a difficulty with something or other in spiritual matters, why don't you go to her? She'll say, "Oh relax. I've had the secret for sixty years. I've only found out now. But it's all yours; what I know now, it's all yours. Let's sit down and talk."

What a strange thing it is that God chose her to be the gate through which he came. But there she is—wide open for us to go through.

The Trinity: Our Family

I was thinking a very simple thought. I thought of the fact that Jesus told us about his Father. It is through his love that we heard about the Father. Abba, Father—how beautiful that we heard it from his own lips. He gave us the prayer, "Our Father who art in heaven"; everything went into it. I don't know if you've felt the way I did when I understood this prayer. I felt I really have a Father. I felt so happy.

Then, as he was dying, nailed to the cross, he couldn't move, but he spoke. He gave us the concept of mother. He told St. John that this was the woman he had to take care of and he told her that she was to take care of him. And in that sentence, he opened motherhood to Mary for everyone: Moslem and Jew, believer and unbeliever, Catholic and Protestant, all are her children (Jn 19:26-7).

So I realized that I also have a mother, a heavenly mother—a Mother and a Father. My joy was great. It is wonderful to have a Father who understands you, who is always there, who is compassionate and good, as God the Father is. It is wonderful to have a mother.

Then I said to myself, "Father, Son, and Holy Spirit." It came to me that the Holy Spirit overshadowed Mary. Every man overshadows his wife. It is through this overshadowing, (the conjugal act), that we are introduced to the Holy Spirit. In my constantly active imagination, I saw myself sitting at the feet of Our Lady, in great peace. For she is a woman wrapped in silence, a woman of peace.

At some point she said, "Catherine, come." She took me by the hand and led me to the Holy Spirit and said, "This is my Spouse." As if struck by a bolt of lightning, beautiful beyond all ability to express, I saw that had a Father, a Brother, and the Holy Spirit who overshadowed her, and I had Our Lady of the Trinity.

Then I thought again, and I said "Here is Father, mother, children. There is a human family and there is a divine family: Father, Son, and Holy Spirit. When the two come together, sanctity surrounds them. Because when the human family merges into the family of God it is sanctified."

Very clearly I saw that there was a Trinity. It stood, as it were, apart, against a flaming sky: the Father, Abba; the Son, and the Holy Spirit.

I realized that this was a true family, the real family, the Heavenly Family. And into the midst of this Heavenly Family entered a woman. What great honor—the word is not really honor at all. It is beyond all honor: this woman who was the daughter of the Father, the mother of the Son, and the spouse of the Holy Spirit, shone with the radiance of all Three.

It is miraculous. It is incredible. But it is the reality of truth. Man becomes one when his family is one with the family of God. When he worships and loves God and understands the connection between the Trinity and Our Lady of the Trinity and himself and his family, the restoration of the family can begin to take place. The link is God our Father, Mary our mother, and Jesus our brother, all of them speaking through the Holy Spirit.

There it was for me to look at. I felt incredibly happy, beyond all ability to express my happiness. I knew within my heart that some day I would have to write about it, because she, my great love, wanted me to do so. She wanted me to present her to her children as the daughter of the Father, mother of the Son, and the one overshadowed by the Holy Spirit. All this I could hold, as it were, in my hands and look at it from inside. Not from the outside, because you don't look at a mystery like that from the outside.

Slowly, quietly, I entered into one mystery after another: the young woman who heard the voice of an angel say, "Hail Mary, full of grace," the woman who remained where she was—laundering, cleaning, keeping house.

The Mystery of Mary

After this I realized something else—the immense mystery that surrounds this woman. So I followed her. I followed her through the Gospel, on a pilgrimage. The further I followed her, the closer I came to her. The strangeness of her mystery became a little clearer to me. My love grew like a fire. I understood the strange mystery of choice. Of all the people in the world, God selected a young Jewish girl to be the mother of his Son.

I understood and yet I didn't understand anything. Neither will you, because mysteries are not meant to be understood. Mysteries are to be believed in. Faith is the footstool of mysteries.

I listened. You can listen with me. As you listen, you will penetrate, little by little, into each mystery. The mysteries of God are overwhelming and to penetrate even a little into any of them is overwhelming. I have no words—neither will you.

Theology is a wonderful science so long as we don't make a god of it. Because we do not know God through theology, even though the meaning of the word *theo-logy* is the knowledge of God. No. The only way that we know God is on our knees, our mind completely empty and put into our heart, our mouth closed. When we are like that, a mystery can slowly, slowly unfold. This requires silence, solitude and so many other things that Our Lady can teach us.

Each one of us is slowly journeying on a real pilgrimage, not with our two feet but with our heart—our heart that walks standing still. On this pilgrimage we begin to enter into the real questions of life—the existence of God, his infinite love, Our Lady's infinite work on our souls.

She Was a Refugee

With Mary on a donkey holding the baby in her arms, occasionally touching the hand of Joseph, the Holy Family wended their way to Egypt.

There were many refugees before them, and certainly many after them, but these three were exceedingly special. They included the Mother of God; the husband of Mary, the foster-father of God; and there was God.

I wonder how she felt? Why do I wonder? Because it seems to me that when I was a refugee from my country with my husband and infant son, I felt as she did. And I think thousands of refugees all over the world have felt as she did. She was torn from her country by an edict. An angel appeared to Joseph, and told him to take his foster-child and the child's mother to Egypt.

Incredibly, there was no room for Jesus Christ in his own country. In a sense, the country rejected him; he was a refugee. He was rejected in his own country. At a very tender age, in the arms of his mother, he was already a forerunner of the millions of refugees who would come after him.

Only God knows the tremendous pain of being a refugee, of being a stranger in a strange land. Millions of refugees never do return to their own land. The only way to find peace and solace is to understand that even in this world we can enter the communion of saints; it is a home belonging to everyone.

At the door, so to speak, of that communion of saints, someone asks, "Have you forgiven all those who hurt you? Have you loved your enemies?" If the answer is in the affirmative, then the doors open wide. You cease to be a refugee, and you belong, now, today, to the communion of saints. (God really meant that we should all be saints. For a saint is simply a person who loves and forgives.)

However, let's look around North America, at all those who come within our shores. If the truth be told, all of us are refugees. This land of plenty once belonged to the Native people alone. But we took it away from them. Since then, we have taken so much away from so many. Oh, we have given refugees poor jobs. We have let them work—for a mere pittance. But, in a way we have killed them, not with kindness, but with hard work that no one else would like to do. Yes, that's the way it used to be and still is.

A Song

There is a woman who has said one word, "fiat," "yes." That word resounded down through the centuries: "Let it be done to me according to your word" (Lk 1:38). You can use that word as a song, constantly, for it is a song that is so pleasing to God.

The fiat of Our Lady is not heard in the land. The will of God is often not done by Christians. Psychiatrists today say that the next generation are going to be maimed spiritually and mentally. And it is true.

We have no tomorrows. One reason we have no tomorrows is that parents of the industrial nations, in a special way the woman, have taken the tomorrows away.

This will not go on, because it's not normal. Our Lady is normal. She stands up there, small, humble, ready to fulfil the will of God, her fiat constantly on her lips, following Christ no matter where he goes, right to the cross.

What happened while she stood at the foot of the cross? Such a simple thing. Jesus turned to her and said that she is the mother of John and that John is her son. That made her the mother of the world: Protestants, Catholics, Muslims, Jews, Gentiles, pagans—all belong to her, all know her in one shape or another. She is the mother of all humankind.

People walk through the door of Madonna House, and are greeted with tenderness, understanding, and all the qualities that a woman gives. When they enter this house, something happens. They are enveloped in the femininity that is Our Lady's. So in a funny, strange way, their pilgrim feet can rest here for a while. They are lost, so many of them. They are lost, perhaps because their mothers weren't able to give what they should have given in tenderness and understanding.

Faintly, if we have ears to hear, we can hear a voice in the distance saying, "Fiat. I have come to do the will of my Father." That is Our Lady.

We need more femininity. We need more simplicity. We need more tenderness—the beautiful tenderness that has nothing to do with sex or anything like it. So someone would approach and say to you: "Come, give me your hand. You are very tired." That's what Our Lady would do. Why don't we?

Now we are ready to speak of Our Lady of Combermere.

*Our Lady
of Combermere*

12

Our Lady of Combermere

In our pursuit of the extraordinary we easily miss the miracle present in the ordinary. The story of Our Lady of Combermere is such a story. Isn't Our Lady most clearly to be found in the ordinariness of our days? The story of Our Lady of Combermere is still unfolding. This is how it begins.

It is a beautiful sunny spring day, a bit cold, but the blue of the Madawaska River sparkles as it did so many years ago, in 1947, when Eddie and I stepped out of our car and came to the front of the house. There is not much change in the lines of the hills on the horizon, nor in the immense tree which stands sentinel where the river narrows, known locally as the Sentinel. We were told then that it was nearly a hundred years old. Well, it has since grown older, but it hasn't changed. I look at the scenery and realize God's infinite goodness to me and the apostolate in the years that have passed since October 15, 1930, the day we began our first foundation.

Those years pass through my memory like rosary beads through the fingers of a child. Each an Alleluia! My heart sings as I write these lines.

Were someone to ask what I consider the most outstanding facts, the most extraordinary graces in our apostolate, I would answer the gifts of Our Lady and of priests.

The chain of events I would select as most unusual is the coming of Our Lady of Combermere. I am tempted to call it a miracle, but I can't; for, unless the Church calls it that officially, we are not allowed to do so. But the faithful are permitted to be grateful, and to speculate on the goodness of God and his mother. For if there is one thing I did not expect, besides the coming of the priests, it was to have Our Lady dwell among us under this musical and dearly familiar name. This is the time and the place to tell you about it.

It began very simply, because in Russia and in many other parts of Europe, women are apt to call on Our Lady by the name of their village, county, river, or by any name they use all the time. I began to invoke her under the title of Our Lady of Combermere. When I set the bread before I went to Mass in the morning, around 5 A.M., I would say, "Our Lady of Combermere, watch over this bread and make it rise." I would talk to her several times a day. When planting seeds, I would ask her blessing on them. Looking after the chickens, I asked her to make them lay more eggs and bigger ones. If I went traveling, or nursing, I would ask her to protect me. It was perfectly natural for me to do so.

How Did It Happen?

In those days we had but five acres of land. Madonna House stood alone, with no buildings around about, not even a woodshed, ice-house, or tool shed.

Those were pioneering days and no mistake! The days of frozen woodpiles covered with a couple feet of snow that had to be brushed off and knocked loose before the sticks could be carried into our tiny kitchen. The days when the paths of snow leading from the front and back doors of Madonna House to the little road that connected us with the rest of the world seemed miles long. There was no fast-rising yeast and bread had to be started the day before. They were days of hard work and many inconveniences, yet glad and joyous days.

Mother of the Ordinary

What could have been more simple and natural when the pumps would not start, and feet and legs were numb from pushing the pedals of the gasoline engine, than to call on Our Lady, giving her the local musical name of Combermere? "Oh please, dear Lady of Combermere, help me to start this washing machine, this pump."

Or again, "Help me to loosen this wood" or "finish this long path in the snow." Or, when the wet wood didn't start burning, as we expected it to, an invocation would easily come to one's lips. Such little prayers are so normal that anyone could understand them. Was this not what I had learned as a child in Russia?

Yes, it was easy to call her affectionately by a familiar, loved name. This is what we did among ourselves, in our apostolic family, thinking nothing of it.

Titles of Our Lady are like endearing names, expressions of great love. Easily we say, "Our Lady of the Kitchen, Our Lady of the Library, Our Lady of the Gardens." So it was with us. So of course we called her "Our Lady of Combermere."

But then things began to happen. In those happenings there was nothing spectacular or extraordinary. They just happened. At first we didn't even notice them happening. It was only when we began to look back that we realized one happening followed another and another.

The first thing that happened was the arrival of a priest friend. He came to visit the apostolate. Casually, he mentioned that he was a student of languages, and that he specialized in archaic, forgotten expressions of our living languages, as well as those of the dead ones.

He asked why our village was named Combermere. We told him what we had heard. It was named after an Englishman, Lord Combermere, whose youngest son, taking the family name of Hudson, settled here way back in the 1790s, having received a grant of land from the English crown.

The priest fastened onto the word *Combermere* itself. He explained to us that the word had a two-fold meaning, and must have come to us through England from France. He said that the first part of the word, *combe,* was a very old French word for "a plateau in the mountains." The second part, the word *mere,* is still in use where French is spoken and means "mother."

So, putting these two words together, one got "Combermere" or, according to him, "mother of a plateau in the mountains."

We were all astonished and delighted because Madonna House is located on a plateau in the mountains! Combermere is about one thousand feet above sea level and lies on a plateau in the foothills of the Laurentian mountains. All around us there are higher mountain peaks of the same Laurentian range.

It was, therefore, wonderful to find out that the affectionate term we had used so often and so naturally really meant that our beloved Lady of Combermere was truly the Mother of our Plateau!

We rested in that knowledge and continued to use our little prayers with more love and gratitude; and Our Lady continued to help us in the needs and chores of our daily living.

Some time later Father Eugene Cullinane brought us a poem about Our Lady of Combermere. Then, on the occasion of the blessing of our original chapel on December 8, 1953, he brought us a song to Our Lady of Combermere, the music for which had been composed by a priest friend of his. We adopted that song, made it our hymn and have sung it ever since.

Time passed. One day a visitor asked if we had thought of how Our Lady of Combermere should look. None of us had. But as the discussion continued, we decided that if we had to draw a picture of Our Lady of Combermere, we would place her near our lovely blue Madawaska River, which flows very close to Madonna House, her arms open in a gesture of welcome and benediction.

Another day a few weeks later the mail brought us a picture of Our Lady drawn by a nun, a Hungarian refugee. It was a nice picture, but not quite what we had imagined Our Lady of Combermere would look like. However, we were glad to have it. We framed the sketch and hung it in a place of honor.

Sometime later Father Cullinane gave us a prayer to go with the picture. It was truly a beautiful prayer. We copied it. So here we were, in a house called Madonna House, all of us totally dedicated to her, praying to her as Our Lady of Combermere, a title never given her before.

One summer a lady came and immediately fell in love with Our Lady of Combermere. She took a supply of the pictures and prayers to her home.

A few months later we received a letter from her saying that she had received a great favor after making a novena to Our Lady of Combermere. In gratitude to her, she wanted to give us a statue, life-sized, preferably in bronze, to be placed outdoors at Madonna House, thus making a shrine to Our Lady of Combermere! She would beg money to get such a statue!

We were quite worried, for we knew that one cannot have a public shrine to Our Lady under a title that has not been approved by Rome. So we wrote to our bishop, Bishop Smith of Pembroke explaining the situation.

He replied that no new title could be used, or funds collected, until the Sacred Congregation of Rites in Rome had been consulted. He said that he would gladly write to the Sacred Congregation concerning this title of Our Lady. He asked us to tell the lady not to start requesting money until the answer came.

We did this, of course, immediately. The lady replied that she would wait; but we were not to worry. Our Lady of Combermere, she was sure, would see that we received a favorable answer—and that it would be soon! (But, we must confess, we did not quite share her faith.)

Great, then, was our astonishment and delight when, in less than two months, we received another letter form our bishop informing us that the Sacred Congregation of Rites had left it to the discretion of the local bishop to approve of the title and statue of Our Lady. The Bishop graciously granted permission to erect a statue of Mary under the title of Our Lady of Combermere and to have it blessed, as well as permission to mint medals in her honor.

Our hearts were singing alleluias, and we were truly overflowing with gratitude. But the question of how Our Lady of Combermere should look remained unsettled. If we were to have a statue, we had to find a sculptor to make it and give him or her an idea of what we wanted. So we prayed. What else could we do?

We prayed and thought and discussed the matter. A large donation of Catholic magazines had come to us and one day we decided to look them over prayerfully. Perhaps we would find in one of them a picture that would strike all of us as the very statue we wanted of Our Lady of Combermere.

The first magazine we opened showed us that statue! There was a photograph of a statue showing Our Lady hastening with arms wide open to welcome and embrace someone, against a wooded background very similar to ours. She seemed to fit right in. Everyone at Madonna House decided this was it.

The picture did not give the name of the sculptor. The caption revealed, however, that the statue was located in Santa Barbara, California, and was called "The Questing Madonna." Well, Our Lady of Combermere was definitely a Questing Madonna in our minds too, for she was the patroness of our apostolate, questing and seeking souls for her Son, which we are trying to do with her.

The sculptor was a woman, a well-known artist, Miss Frances Rich of that city. We wrote to Miss Rich. We were afraid that such a great artist's fees would be beyond our ability to pay. So we told her very frankly how the whole thing came about and how we selected her statue.

To our astonishment and joy, Miss Rich graciously waived any fee for herself. She loved the story of Our Lady of Combermere. She felt very happy, she said, to be able to bring her to Combermere. All she asked was the price of casting it in bronze from her model. This work had to be done in Florence, Italy where the craftsmanship was perfect. We would also pay the shipping charges.

We agreed at once, although we didn't have the money. We felt sure that if Our Lady of Combermere wanted to come here, she would provide it. We started a burse in her honor, and the money was there when it was needed.

Arrival and Blessing

The statue arrived in Combermere on April 26, 1960, and was erected, on top of three thousand pounds of cement, on May 17, the thirteenth anniversary of the opening of Madonna House. Three weeks later, on June 8, 1960, the Bishop came and officially installed and blessed the statue. It was an awesome moment for all of us. Eddie Doherty described it in our newspaper, *Restoration,* as follows:

"The newest shrine in Christendom—and the humblest and least pretentious—was blessed on June 8.

"Combermere is a mere crossroads village lost in the vastness of this Canadian province, a town forgotten or ignored by most of the map-makers, a community that has seldom boasted more than a few hundred people. But perhaps Our Lady loves the humble places like Fatima and Lourdes and a hundred other shrines.

"It was no miracle that produced this shrine. There was no spectacular occurrence of any kind. It was only the coming of a beautiful statue and perhaps the love of the people in and around Madonna House that caused it to become a place of devotion and of pilgrimage.

"The bishop read and sang the words of the blessing. He sprinkled the statue with holy water. He sent the fragrant smoke of incense up and around it, using the ritual fashioned for him many hundreds of years ago. Then he said, along with everyone present, the prayer to Our Lady of Combermere that the people of Madonna House had been saying every day for years.

"When he had finished this prayer he turned and faced the congregation. He was standing before the statue, between its wide-flung arms, and beneath its tender, loving face. He spoke of his first visit to Madonna House, on August 15, 1945, the feast of Our Lady's Assumption, the day of the announcement of the end of the Second World War—the day also when the idea of an apostolate here was conceived.

"'I gave verbal approbation to the work,' he said, 'and later a formal one for this house to be the headquarters of the lay apostolate and the rural apostolate. Of course nobody then envisioned what the future would hold. I did not realize that in so few years such great things would be accomplished here.

"'This afternoon in this very blessed part of the diocese, in this very beautiful part of the world, in this month of June, I know that, as the years go by, great graces will flow out all over this diocese, all over Canada and the United States, and all over the rest of the world through Our Lady of Combermere and the great work to which these people have dedicated their lives.

"'In blessing the statue of Our Lady of Combermere I have in mind the thought that a great deal of the work necessary to bring the world to the feet of Our Lady will depend on the loyalty and devotion of the friends of Combermere. There has been much progress here. The hand of God is in it. We hope that God will continue, through the hands of Our Blessed Mother, the dispenser of all graces, to bless this hallowed spot.

"'We seem to be living in a confused world, one becoming more confused all the time. As the years go by, it seems to me that the solution to the things troubling us will be cared for by Our Lady. She promised to help us, so long as we do our part. So if we listen to her words, in whatever work we do, and dedicate ourselves to her, we will have an opportunity to make recompense to God for many of the sins of the world.

"'Now we bless and dedicate the diocese, and the country, and all the Americas to Our Lady of Combermere. Graces will go out in abundance from Our Lady of Combermere and we shall all benefit from this center of the lay apostolate—all of us—we in the diocese and those outside.'"

For Catherine this was a moment set apart as a beacon of light. She describes it:

I knew many laypeople and clergy were present. I knew that the day was beautiful, sunny and clear, that the garden was beginning to flower, that our choir sang the beautiful hymn of Our Lady of Combermere. All this I knew, and yet in a manner of speaking, I did not know it. I seemed to be suspended between heaven and earth with the joy of it all! I seemed to be in the present and in the past.

Well I knew that I was in the garden of Madonna House, participating in a beautiful and significant ceremony. And yet, it seemed that I was back in 1930, putting my scant belongings in the car of a good friend who was to drive me to Portland Street in Toronto. Only a few blocks from where I had been living, yet a journey beyond measure. For I was moving from comfortable quarters to the slums of that beautiful city, henceforth to serve, to live, to work, and to love—with the poor—who were so numerous in that year of 1930, on that cold day of October, the beginning of the Great Depression.

I realized, of course that I was standing in the grounds of Madonna House beholding a most beautiful statue of Our Lady, hearing the music of an age-old blessing. But somehow, (I do not know how), I was carried to Rochester Street in Ottawa, opening yet another foundation to feed the cold and hungry men, the transients, so numerous in the year 1934 in the capital of Canada.

Then, without transition, as it happens sometime to human beings, I was walking the streets of Harlem, streets that barely boasted a tree, surrounded by swarming kids and men and women with tired faces, going, going, going towards 135th Street and our foundation in that city.

Then Chicago and Marathon City came out of nowhere and engulfed me. I was again at our house in Chicago, amidst poverty and discrimination; then with young blacks at a summer camp at our farm in Marathon City, Wisconsin, amid many youngsters with white teeth flashing and joy in their every movement.

How is it possible to be in one place, and at the same time in so many others? How is it possible to stand still and travel across the span of thirty years since the foundation of our humble apostolate?

The ceremony was finished. The words of the Bishop fell into my heart like pearls of immense price, to be cherished forever. But they were more than pearls. They were wine and oil, balm on long-standing and deep wounds. For journeys the like of which I had made in an instant, but in reality had lasted thirty years, are truly long ones. They are journeys of the spirit, not only of the flesh. And one cannot come out of them unscathed. I did not come out of them unscathed.

Often it seemed I was left lying on strange and dusty roads. Often it seemed I was left bleeding and wounded, "beset by robbers," but always the Lord seems to have lifted me up, and put me to rest in the inn of his most Sacred Heart.

Outstretched Arms

Then all of that was past, and I was standing again under the outstretched hands of Our Lady of Combermere. Bishop Smith, a messenger of love, was healing wounds of long standing with every word.

Yes, I was back from a journey that no one can ever describe. I was standing on the beautiful grounds of Madonna House, with a heart so filled with gratitude and joy that it seemed to me it would stop for the sheer weight of both! But it didn't! It went on beating, fast and joyfully, singing alleluia!

Yes, there are moments in all human lives that stand out as beacons of light, always to be remembered, never forgotten, with a sense of indescribable joy and sometimes, just an indescribable, awe. For our little apostolate, that June 8 will always be such a day.

A booklet with more details about Our Lady of Combermere is available from Madonna House Publications.

Other Writings by
Catherine de Hueck Doherty

Apostolic Farming
Dearly Beloved — 3 volumes
Dear Father
Dear Parents
Dear Seminarian
Donkey Bells
Doubts, Loneliness, Rejection
Faith
Fragments of My Life
The Gospel of a Poor Woman
The Gospel Without Compromise
Grace in Every Season
Journey Inward
Lubov
Molchanie
My Heart and I
My Russian Yesterdays
Not Without Parables
O Jesus
Our Lady's Unknown Mysteries
The People of the Towel and the Water
Poustinia
Season of Mercy
Sobornost
Soul of My Soul
Strannik
Urodivoi
Welcome, Pilgrim

Available from: Madonna House Publications
Combermere, Ontario, Canada
K0J 1L0